WILLA CATHER

LIVES OF NOTABLE GAY MEN AND LESBIANS

WILLA CATHER

SHARON O'BRIEN

MARTIN B. DUBERMAN, General Editor

CHELSEA HOUSE PUBLISHERS ■ New York • Philadelphia

CHELSEA HOUSE PUBLISHERS
EDITORIAL DIRECTOR   Richard Rennert
EXECUTIVE MANAGING EDITOR   Karyn Gullen Browne
COPY CHIEF   Robin James
PICTURE EDITOR   Adrian G. Allen
ART DIRECTOR   Robert Mitchell
MANUFACTURING DIRECTOR   Gerald Levine

LIVES OF NOTABLE GAY MEN AND LESBIANS
SENIOR EDITOR   Sean Dolan
SERIES DESIGN   Basia Niemczyc

Staff for **WILLA CATHER**
ASSISTANT EDITOR   Mary B. Sisson
DESIGNER   M. Cambraia Magalhães
PICTURE RESEARCHER   Pat Burns
COVER ILLUSTRATION   Bonnie Gardner

Introduction copyright © 1994 by Martin B. Duberman.

Text copyright © 1995 by Chelsea House Publishers, a division of Main Line Book Co. All rights reserved. Printed and bound in the United States of America.

First Printing

1 3 5 7 9 8 6 4 2

Library of Congress Cataloging-in-Publication Data

O'Brien, Sharon.
Willa Cather / Sharon O'Brien; introduction by Martin B. Duberman.
p. cm.—(Lives of notable gay men and lesbians)
Includes bibliographical references and index.
ISBN 0-7910-2302-8
     0-7910-2877-1 (pbk.)
1. Cather, Willa, 1873–1947—Biography—Juvenile literature. 2. Women novelists, American—20th century—Biography—Juvenile literature. 3. Lesbians—United States—Biography—Juvenile literature. [1. Cather, Willa, 1873–1947. 2. Authors, American. 3. Lesbians—Biography.] I. Title. II. Series.
PS3505.A87Z746 1994
813'.52—dc20   93-43244
[B]   CIP
                                                                  AC

CONTENTS

Gay, Straight, and in Between *Martin Duberman*		7
Author's Preface *Sharon O'Brien*		15
1	THE HERO OF HER OWN STORY	21
2	FROM VIRGINIA TO NEBRASKA	29
3	"THE THING NOT NAMED"	47
4	THE EMERGING VOICE	67
5	EVERY ARTIST MAKES HERSELF BORN	89
6	THE WRITING LIFE	113
Books by Willa Cather		138
Further Reading		139
Chronology		140
Index		142

Titles in
◈ LIVES OF NOTABLE GAY MEN AND LESBIANS ◈

Jane Addams	Audre Lorde
Alvin Ailey	Carson McCullers
James Baldwin	Harvey Milk
Willa Cather	Gabriela Mistral
Marlene Dietrich	Martina Navratilova
E. M. Forster	Mary Renault
Federico García Lorca	Bayard Rustin
Lorraine Hansberry	Sappho
Edith Head	Bessie Smith
Rock Hudson	Gertrude Stein
Elton John	Andy Warhol
John Maynard Keynes	Walt Whitman
K. D. Lang	Oscar Wilde
T. E. Lawrence	Tennessee Williams
Liberace	Virginia Woolf

Gay, Straight, and in Between

by Martin Duberman

Being different is never easy. Especially in a culture like ours, which puts a premium on conformity and equates difference with deficiency. And especially during the teenage years when one feels desperate for acceptance and vulnerable to judgment. If you are taller or shorter than average, or fatter or thinner, or physically challenged, or of the "wrong" color, gender, religion, nationality, or sexual orientation, you are likely to be treated as "less than," as inferior to what the majority has decreed is the optimal, standard model.

Theoretically, those of us who are different should be delighted that we are *not* ordinary, not just another cookie-cutter product of mainstream culture. We should glory in the knowledge that many remarkably creative figures, past and present, are people who lived outside accepted norms and pressed hard against accepted boundaries.

But in reality many of us have internalized the majority's standards of worth, and we do not feel very good about ourselves. How could we? When we look around us, we see that most people in high places of visibility, privilege, and power are white, heterosexual males of a very traditional kind. That remains true even though intolerance may have ebbed *somewhat* in recent decades and people of diverse backgrounds may have *begun* to attain more of a foothold in our culture.

Many gay men and lesbians through time have looked and acted like "ordinary" people and could therefore choose to "stay in the closet" and avoid social condemnation—though the effort at concealment produced its own turmoil and usually came at the price of self-acceptance. On the other hand, "sissy" gay men or "butch" lesbians have been quickly categorized and scorned by the mainstream culture as "sexual deviants"—even though no necessary link exists between gender nonconformity and sexual orientation. In the last 15 years or so, however, more and more people who previously would have passed as straight *have* been choosing to "come out." They sense that social consequences are no longer as severe as they once were—and that the psychic costs of concealment are taking too great a toll.

Yet even today, there are comparatively few role models available for gays and lesbians to emulate. And unlike other oppressed minorities, homosexuals don't often find confirmation within their own families. Even when a homosexual child is not rejected outright, acceptance comes within a family unit that is structurally heterosexual and in which homosexuality is generally mocked and decried. With his or her different desire and experience, the gay son or lesbian daughter remains an exotic. Moreover, such children are unable to find in family lore and traditions—as other minority people can—a compensatory source of validation to counterbalance the ridicule of mainstream culture.

Things are rarely any better at school, where textbooks and lessons are usually devoid of relevant information about homosexuality. Nor does the mainstream culture—movies or television, for example—often provide gays or lesbians with positive images of themselves, let alone any sense of historical antecedents. These silences are in large measure a reflection of the culture's homophobia. But to a lesser degree they reflect two other matters as well: the fact that many accomplished gay men and lesbians in the past refused to publicly acknowledge their sexuality (sometimes even to themselves); and secondly, the problem of assigning "gay" or "lesbian" identities to past figures who lived at a time when those conceptual categories did not exist.

For the surprising finding of recent scholarship is that categorizing human beings on the basis of sexual desire alone is a relatively recent phenomenon of the last several hundred years. It is a development, many historians believe, tied to the increasing urbanization of Europe and the Americas, and to the new opportunities city life presented for anonymity—for freedom from the relentless scrutiny of family and neighbors that had characterized farming communities and small towns. Only with the new freedom afforded by city life, historians are telling us, could people who felt they were different give free rein to their natures, lay claim to a distinctive identity, and begin to elaborate a subculture that would reflect it.

Prior to, say, 1700 (the precise date is under debate), the descriptive categories of "straight" or "gay" were not widely employed in dividing up human nature. Even today, in many non-Western parts of the world, it is unusual to categorize people on the basis of sexual orientation alone. Through time and across cultures it has often been assumed that *both* same- and opposite-gender erotic feelings (what we now call "bisexuality") could coexist in an individual—even if *acting* on same-gender impulses was usually taboo.

In the West, where we *do* currently divide humanity into separate, oppositional categories of *gay* and *straight,* most people grow up accepting that division as "natural" and dutifully assign themselves to one category or the other. Those who adopt the definition *gay* or *lesbian,* however, soon discover that mainstream culture offers homosexuals (unlike heterosexuals) no history or sense of forebears. This is a terrible burden, especially during the teenage years, when one is actively searching for a usable identity, for a continuum in which to place oneself and lay claim to a contented and productive life.

This series is designed, above all, to fill that huge, painful cultural gap. It is designed to instill not only pride in antecedents but encouragement, the kind of encouragement that literature and biography have always provided: proof that someone else out there has felt what we have felt, experienced what we have experienced, been where we have been—and has endured, achieved, and flourished.

But *who* to include in this series has been problematic. Even today, many people refuse to define themselves as gay or lesbian. In some cases, they do not wish to confine what they view as their fluid sexuality into narrow, either/or categories. In other cases, they may acknowledge to themselves that their sexuality does fit squarely within the gay category, yet refuse to say so publicly, unwilling to take on the onus of a lesbian or gay identity. In still other cases, an individual's sense of sexual identity can change during his or her lifetime, as can his or her sense of its importance, when compared with many other strands, in defining their overall temperament.

Complicating matters still further is the fact that even today—when multitudes openly call themselves gay or lesbian, and when society as a whole argues about gay marriage and parenting or the place of gay people in the military—there is still no agreed-upon definition of what centrally constitutes a gay or lesbian identity. Should we call someone gay if his or her sexual desire is *predominantly* directed toward people of his or her own gender? But then how do we establish predominance? And by *desire* do we mean actual behavior—or fantasies that are never acted out? (Thus Father John McNeill, the writer and Jesuit, has insisted—though he has never actually had sex with another man—that on the basis of his erotic fantasies, he *is* a gay man.)

Some scholars and theorists even argue that genital sexuality need not be present in a relationship before we can legitimately call it gay or lesbian, stressing instead the central importance of same-gender *emotional* commitment. The problem of definition is then further complicated when we include the element of *self*-definition. If we come across someone in the past who does not explicitly self-identify as gay, by what right, and according to what evidence, can we legitimately claim them anyway?

Should we eliminate all historical figures who lived before *gay* or *lesbian* were available categories for understanding and ordering their experience? Are we entitled, for the purposes of this series, to include at least some of those from the past whose sexuality seems not to have been confined to one gender or the other, or who—as a cover to protect a public image or a career—may have married, and thus have been commonly taken to be heterosexual? And if we do not include some of those whose sexuality cannot be clearly categorized as *gay,* then how can we speak of a gay and lesbian continuum, a *history*?

In deciding which individuals to include in *Notable Gay Men and Lesbians,* I have gone back and forth between these competing definitions, juggling, combining, and, occasionally, finessing them. For the most part, I have tried to confine my choices to those figures who *by any definition* (same-gender emotional commitment, erotic fantasy, sexual behavior, *and* self-definition) do clearly qualify for inclusion.

But alas, we often lack the needed intimate evidence for such clear-cut judgments. I have regretfully omitted from the series many bisexual figures, and especially the many well-known women—Tallulah Bankhead, Judy Garland, Greta Garbo, Josephine Baker, for example—whose erotic and emotional preference seems indeterminable (usually for lack of documentation). But I will probably include a few—Margaret Mead, say, or Marlene Dietrich—as witnesses to the difficult ambiguities of sexual definition, and to allow for a discussion of those ambiguities.

In any case, I suspect much of the likely criticism over this or that choice will come from those eager to conceal their distaste for a series devoted to "Notable (no less!) Gay Men and Lesbians" under the guise of protesting a single inclusion or omission within it. That kind of criticism can be easily borne, and is more than compensated for, by the satisfaction of acquainting today's young gays and lesbians—and indeed all who feel "different"—with some of those distinguished forebears whose existence can inform and comfort them.

Sharon O'Brien's rich, subtle biography of Willa Cather beautifully illustrates, along with much else, some of the definitional problems I have referred to above. Why is a figure like Cather—reticent about her private life and reluctant to assume any one-dimensional label—in a series clearly demarked *Notable Gay Men and Lesbians*? Having deliberately destroyed personal correspondence to shield her life from prying eyes, even retroactive ones, would not Cather herself have been outraged at her inclusion here?

Perhaps. But since she did not live in these more permissive times, the answer must be uncertain. Besides, the wishes of the dead, even when they are clear (and with Cather they are not) cannot always take precedence. The life of a major literary figure like Cather inevitably becomes the subject of analysis, and the biographer's only reliable guide must be to "tell the whole truth." Of course the truth is not always obvious or available, nor is it unshaded. And the brilliance of Sharon O'Brien's account of Cather lies in the careful and astute discriminations of her portrait.

The Willa Cather who emerges from this volume is what O'Brien calls "a cultural outsider." Growing up in a society with sharply defined gender roles, she refused to confine herself, either as writer or human being, to the traditional female sphere. As a writer, Cather rejected the "female" genre of sentimental domestic fiction; and as a human being, she refused to live her life as a docile satellite to a man. She insisted on finding her own voice, and it turned out to be a powerfully individual one, assertive and confident—all that her culture labeled "masculine." And in her personal life, Cather looked to women, not men, for intimacy and support. It took great courage thus to challenge her society's set definitions of what it did and should mean to be a woman, to live outside accepted boundaries.

We know literally nothing about the details of Cather's erotic life, nothing, for example, about which, if any, of her romantic attachments to women included the element of genital sexuality (though O'Brien does make the telling point that "Given the understanding of sexual passion she shows in her fiction . . . she understood sexual desire very well, and from experience . . ."). Of course we rarely have detailed information about the sexual feelings and experiences of *any* historical figure, whether "gay" or "straight."

What *is* indisputable is that Cather's world was almost entirely homosocial. Her closest connections were with women, her passion and solicitude largely confined to them; at every period of her life, whether deeply in love with Isabelle McClung or for 30 years sharing a home with Edith Lewis, Cather's emotional life centered on other women. As O'Brien makes clear, Cather was well aware that such intense bonds between women were being increasingly stigmatized by mainstream culture as "unnatural," as they had not been for much of the 19th century.

(As a young woman Cather had even used that pejorative word to characterize her own romantic feelings for Louise Pound.)

Does all this entitle us to call Willa Cather a "lesbian"? Most of her biographers have skirted the question, or consigned Cather to the ranks of the celibate or asexual. But Sharon O'Brien has compellingly insisted that Cather *was* a lesbian—and that her sexuality, moreover, is of central importance in understanding her creative process and her fiction (an argument summarized by Cather's own phrase about the "inexpressible presence of the thing not named" being at the heart of fiction's true power).

At the same time O'Brien warns us against any glib equation of Cather's lesbianism with the whole of her being: it was one strand in a complex personality. As O'Brien shrewdly comments, "The problem is ours, really: once we apply the category *homosexual* or *lesbian* to someone, that sexual identity may be all we can see."

Author's Preface

Willa Cather did not make it easy for her biographers. In the last years of her life, she destroyed the letters in her possession and wrote a will in which she forbade quotation from her correspondence. Like many writers, Cather wanted to protect her privacy, and she did not trust future biographers and critics to address her life or her work sympathetically.

But Willa Cather had another reason for wanting to guard her private life. Judging from her letters, she was willing to be viewed as a woman, but not as a lesbian. Her love for women was a source of great strength and imaginative power to her, but she feared misunderstanding and repudiation if this love were to be publicly named—quite a legitimate fear in her time. But since I am writing in a more enlightened era than hers, I can assume that I am addressing the sympathetic readers that Cather, given her historical moment, could not have imagined.

I am still aware that Willa Cather would not have approved of my writing a biography that mentions her lesbianism. When I was working on my full-length biography of her, *Willa Cather: The Emerging Voice,* I knew that scholarly integrity required me to explore the connections between sexuality and creativity; but I still felt some guilt about venturing into personal territory that she wanted to guard. One night, I dreamed that Cather invited me to tea in her Greenwich Village apartment. Pouring me a cup from her silver teapot, she turned to me and said, "I just want you to know that I'm not gay." Ever the biographer, I stood my ground and asked, "What about the letters to Louise Pound [Cather's first lover]?" She did not reply, and the dream ended. Later, my anxiety surfaced again: I dreamed that Edith Lewis, Cather's longtime companion, called me up and said, "I just want you to keep the word 'lesbian' out of the biography." Of course, I could not promise I would, and she hung up.

Finally, though, Willa Cather and I came to a reconciliation, at least in my unconscious. As I was finishing up the manuscript, I dreamed I was a guest in her house. She came downstairs with my bags packed—not a gesture of rejection but a sign of a considerate hostess. It was time for me to go.

As these dreams suggest, writing a biography is not just an intellectual experience. The biographer forms a close emotional and imaginative relationship with the subject, and at times that relationship may seem more real, more intense, than bonds with people in one's daily life. All in all, I spent 15 years on my full-length biography of Willa Cather, and when it was finished I thought I would never want to write about her again.

I changed my mind when I was asked to write a biography for readers in a series to be called *Lives of Notable Gay Men and Lesbians*. I thought that the series was needed, and the publisher was brave and imaginative to create it. I also thought that Cather's life—itself filled with bravery and imagination—had much to offer readers in their teens and early twenties, a period of difficult transition when we all need hopeful stories to help us grow up.

Although novels such as *My Ántonia* and stories such as "Paul's Case" are now frequently taught in high schools, paradoxically Willa Cather did not want her fiction to be read in high school. She did everything she could during her lifetime to limit the dissemination of her fiction. She controlled the excerpts from her fiction that could appear in anthologies and refused permission to anthologies intended for use in high schools. She successfully kept all her novels out of paperback and prevailed upon Houghton Mifflin, her publisher, not to sell *My Ántonia* to the movies. As the publisher Alfred Knopf recalls, Cather did not want her books to be read in the classroom because she feared that if readers were exposed to her in a coercive, authoritarian environment, they might "grow up hating her." In other words, she did not want to be on reading lists, syllabi, or tests.

Cather resisted being "taught" to students because her view of the ideal relationship between writer and reader was based on the model of friendship. She wanted readers to respond voluntarily and imaginatively to her work because her writing struck some chord of affection in them. "When we find ourselves on shipboard, among hundreds of strangers," she wrote, "we very soon recognize those who are sympathetic to us. We like a writer much as we like individuals; for what he is, simply, underneath his accomplishments." But if her novels were assigned, then the relationship between the reader and the text would be enforced, not freely chosen. To follow out the implications of her metaphor, reading a writer in the classroom would be like a hostage forming a bond with a captor, not like a traveler striking up a shipboard friendship.

So strongly did Cather wish readers to discover her fiction independently that throughout the 1920s she refused to allow her novels to be adopted by book clubs. She relented only with *Shadows on the Rock*, in part responding to the private claims of friendship: Dorothy Canfield Fisher, then one of the judges of the Book-of-the-Month Club, prevailed upon her.

After Cather's death, Edith Lewis, who became executor of her estate, agreed finally to paperback editions, and Cather's fiction has long been taught in high schools. So it is certainly possible that some of you reading this biography have encountered Willa Cather because her work has been assigned to you. You may have been required to write a paper on her work or to take an examination in which questions were asked about *My Ántonia*. So you may not have yet approached Willa Cather freely, as a literary friend.

But friendship can often develop after assigned meetings. Such was the case for me. I read *My Ántonia* in high school because I had to, and then I forgot all about Willa Cather. I associated her with conservatism and Catholicism because my Irish Catholic father kept telling me I should read *Death Comes for the Archbishop* and *Shadows on the Rock*—a sure way to keep Cather off my reading list. When I was in graduate school, during the early years of the women's movement, I complained to a friend that American fiction was terribly hard on strong women. "I'm tired of reading books where women end up dead or punished," I said. "Try Willa Cather," he said.

So I read O *Pioneers!* and found a new literary world opening to me: here was a writer who could imagine a female character as creative and strong, and who didn't end the novel by making her heroine walk into the ocean. I also fell in love with Cather's lucid, evocative, pure style. Having spent too much time wandering in the convoluted prose of Henry James's late novels—brilliant writing, of course, but not my cup of tea—I found entering Cather's verbal landscape the equivalent of leaving a labyrinth for the thrilling openness of the Nebraska plains.

I wrote my dissertation on Cather and then spent 10 years writing a biography. In my work, I could write about issues that concerned me deeply—gender, sexuality, the creative process—and still be in the company of a writer whose prose made me happy. For the first time, I felt that my private and public worlds might come together, that I might be able to teach and write what I cared about. So my literary friendship with Cather allowed me to stay in graduate school (I'd been on the verge of leaving) and become a teacher and a writer.

I hope, then, that if you have encountered Willa Cather in the classroom, you can hold open the possibility of developing a literary friendship with her—if not now, perhaps sometime in the future. I still turn back to her fiction for inspiration and guidance; sometimes she is a friend, sometimes a mentor, sometimes the voice of my best self. One passage from *My Ántonia* I read and reread, and quote to anyone who will listen. It's the beautiful section in which Jim is lying drowsily in the garden, surrounded by yellowing pumpkins and ladybugs, and it leads to the quotation that Cather wanted on her gravestone:

> The earth was warm under me, and warm as I crumbled it through my fingers. Queer little red bugs came out and moved in slow squadrons around me. Their backs were polished vermilion, with black spots. I kept as still as I could. Nothing happened. I did not expect anything to happen. I was something that

lay under the sun and felt it, like the pumpkins, and I did not want to be anything more. I was entirely happy. Perhaps we feel like that when we die and become a part of something entire, whether it is sun and air, or goodness and knowledge. At any rate, that is happiness; to be dissolved into something complete and great. When it comes to one, it comes as naturally as sleep.

Whenever I become enmeshed in that curse of American life, a narcissistic preoccupation with myself and my accomplishments (or lack thereof), I like to say to myself "that is happiness; to be dissolved into something complete and great." Cather's voice helps remind me of the pleasure that can come from leaving the self behind, "dissolving" as I place my attention outward on my students, or my friends, or the words that flow from my fountain pen. (Like Cather, I do first drafts by hand.)

I am grateful to Cather for those words, for the literary friendship we have had, and for the novels she has left us. I am also glad that her work is available in paperback and taught in high schools. According to Cather, a fine writer leaves in the mind of the receptive reader a "cadence, a quality of voice that is exclusively the writer's own, individual, unique." Perhaps some of you have heard Cather's distinctive voice speaking to you even from within the structure of a classroom or a syllabus, and you will some day begin an enriching friendship with her. If so, as a reader you will receive the emotional and spiritual connection with a writer that Willa Cather, speaking of her own literary friendship with Sarah Orne Jewett, called "a gift from heart to heart."

CHAPTER ONE

THE HERO OF HER OWN STORY

"The books we read when we were children shaped our lives, at least they shaped our imaginings, and it is with our imaginings that we live," the novelist Willa Cather once observed. Like those of other girls who grew up in 19th-century America, Cather's childhood and adolescent imaginings were shaped by stories clearly marked "male" or "female." Books supposedly for boys, such as *Treasure Island* and *Captains Courageous,* were tales of adventure in which the male hero overcomes obstacles and attains self-reliance and power. Books for girls, such as *Little Women,* center on the private world of domesticity and emotion, and the heroine ultimately attains feminine success when she either dies—like the piously ailing sister Beth—or prepares for marriage and motherhood, like Meg, Amy, and even the tomboy Jo.

As a young reader, Willa Cather scorned the heroine's plot, which she associated with what she called

Frustrated with the passive and uninteresting roles available to young women in Victorian America, the adolescent Willa Cather cropped her hair short, wore men's clothing, and renamed herself William.

WILLA CATHER

"namby-pamby" femininity. She preferred to identify with the heroes of boys' stories, who possessed the autonomy and self-determination she wanted for herself. Her reading choices were not unusual: many girls found the stirring action of boys' books more interesting reading than the domestic niceness of girls' books. But all girls were expected, no matter what their reading, to conform to the expected female role

Cather claimed that she had been named after William Boak, an uncle and a Confederate soldier who died during the Civil War, and she often wore military garb to emulate him. In reality, she had been baptized Wilella after her father's sister, a fact she tried to disguise by replacing Wilella with Willa in the family Bible.

22

THE HERO OF HER OWN STORY

when they reached adolescence. According to 19th-century ideology, then they were to develop the qualities of "true womanhood": purity, piety, submissiveness, and domesticity. Most girls did conform to social pressures, abandoning tomboy childhoods for the realms Victorian advice books thought appropriate for women—the "washroom, the kitchen, and the garden"—where they would learn properly self-sacrificing female behavior.

Such girls would be accepting their society's definition of appropriate gender roles, which divided boys and girls into separate groups and gave them separate destinies. While *sex* signifies the biological difference between men and women, *gender* signifies the socially defined categories of "masculine" and "feminine." Dominant conceptions of what is masculine or feminine may seem natural and inevitable to people living within a culture, but in fact these conceptions are socially fashioned and can differ over time and across cultures. In the Victorian period, when Willa Cather came of age, gender roles were strongly polarized—while women were granted the private realm of delicate emotions and domestic tranquillity, men were awarded the larger and more prestigious public world of assertive self-expression and individual achievement.

This expansive and supposedly masculine world seemed far more attractive to Willa Cather than the kitchen, washroom, or garden, and so she devised a defiant response to her society's expectation that she conform to the heroine's plot. Instead of becoming a character in someone else's narrative, she turned herself into the hero of her own life story by becoming William Cather: she cut her hair to crew-cut length and adopted boyish dress. Photographs show her in a soldierly costume with Civil War cap; with a coat, tie, and derby hat; and with shirtwaist dress and boater hat. Sometimes she signed her name "William Cather, jr.," and at others "William Cather, M.D.," when she wanted to let people know she wanted to be a doctor, not a wife.

Unconsciously, Willa Cather sensed what contemporary feminist and cultural theorists are telling us: that gender is not innate, but is a kind of social performance. Her dramatic flair carried over to the actual stage, and she played the role of the father in a children's performance of

WILLA CATHER

Young Willa (back row, center, with hat) poses with the cast of a neighborhood production of *Beauty and the Beast*. Cather's love for theater—especially its drama, flair, and flamboyant costumes—extended throughout her adult life and found expression in stories such as "Paul's Case."

Beauty and the Beast. She was so convincing that one member of the audience refused to believe she was a girl.

Cather's unorthodox dress and manner, played out on the stage of Red Cloud, Nebraska, brought her "considerable notoriety" and made her the subject of "much talk around town," remembered Elmer Thomas, a contemporary who viewed her performance from a safe distance. Cather was impervious to criticism, he recalled, and "even boasted that she preferred the masculine garb" as well as the masculine

THE HERO OF HER OWN STORY

sex. Thomas was disconcerted by his cross-dressing neighbor. "I remember her mostly for her boyish makeup and the serious stare with which she met you. It was as if she said, 'Stay your distance buddy, I have your number.' Enough, I did."

Cather was not interested in attracting the Elmer Thomases of Red Cloud, and she was not going to silence herself to appease what she called "the tongue of gossip" in *My Ántonia*. In that novel, she describes how a small town's narrow, conservative society could damage the full expression of the self: "The guarded mode of existence was like living under a tyranny. People's speech, their voices, their very glances, became furtive and repressed. Every individual taste, every natural appetite, was bridled by caution. The people asleep in those houses, I thought, tried . . . to make no noise, to leave no trace, to slip over the surface of things in the dark."

If we had known Willa Cather at the time she became William, of course we could not have said, "That young woman is destined to become a great writer." In retrospect, however, we can see the connection between Cather's discovery of her vocation as an artist and her youthful male impersonation. The most obvious connection is her willingness to transgress boundaries and to enter territories where women were not supposed to go. In the late 19th and early 20th centuries, *woman* and *artist* were incompatible categories, so when she became a serious writer, Cather was also refusing to follow the heroine's plot.

In the flair of her male performance—her delight in costume, dress, appearance—we can also see the future novelist's power to invent a world and to project the self into all kinds of characters—male, female, heterosexual, homosexual, young, old, native-born, immigrant. The artist must be a "chameleon," as the poet John Keats observed, able to take on different identities. The chameleon Willa/William Cather agreed, saying there was no greater delight for her than "entering into another person's skin."

Her William Cather performance also shows her bravery, a quality a writer needs: for it is the writers who take personal and aesthetic risks, rather than those who conform to literary and social conventions, whose work endures. As a teenager, the stage of life when most of us are most vulnerable to outside opinion, Cather was willing to risk criticism and perhaps ostracism because she did not want to silence herself.

Had Cather come of age in America in the late 20th century, she might not have needed to adopt a male identity when she reached adolescence. Even though our patriarchal society still socializes us into the separate and unequal categories of male and female, there are more opportunities for women now—a wider variety of life stories—than there were in Victorian America, when gender roles were so rigidly differentiated. In the 1880s, it seemed to Cather that there were only two choices: active or passive, independent or dominated, male or female. True womanhood seemed inconsistent with personhood, so the young Willa Cather chose masculinity.

Ultimately, however, Willa Cather would leave William Cather behind and find a way to integrate the identities of woman and artist. As long as she repudiated women she was repudiating herself, and denial is never a powerful source of creativity. Had Cather never moved beyond male identification, she would not have become the writer we read today, a writer who has given us a variety of memorable female characters as well as male characters, a writer who does not imitate male writers but who speaks in her own voice.

In her adult years, Willa Cather revised the William Cather plot and invented a new story for herself, a story in which she could dress the way she wanted, form friendships with both women and men, have primary emotional partnerships with women and business relationships and friendships with men, and become a writer whose life and work was neither conventionally feminine nor conventionally masculine but was her own.

How did she shape this unconventional life story? Where did she find the inspiration, guidance, friendship, love, and community that supported her solitary journey away from the masculine and the feminine plot? How did she discover and experience her love for women, and what impact did her emotional choices have on her writing? How did her life shape her fiction, and how in turn did her artistic vocation shape her life? And what value might her life and work have for us?

As we trace Cather's evolution as woman and artist, we will also explore these questions. The place to begin is Back Creek, Virginia, the small farming community where Willa Cather was born in 1873, only eight years after the close of the Civil War.

CHAPTER TWO

FROM VIRGINIA TO NEBRASKA

Like many Victorian children, Cather was encouraged to take on dramatic roles and make recitations. Here she gives a dramatic reading of Henry Wadsworth Longfellow's *The Song of Hiawatha*; her performance led a Red Cloud, Nebraska, paper to compliment her "elocutionary powers" and her "extraordinary self-control and talent."

"I shall never forget," Willa Cather said, "my introduction to [Nebraska]. . . . The land was open range and there was almost no fencing. As we drove further and further out into the country I felt a good deal as if we had come to the end of everything—it was a kind of erasure of personality."

Although we associate Cather with the sweeping, fertile land of the Nebraska Divide she evokes in novels such as *O Pioneers!, My Ántonia,* and *A Lost Lady,* she spent her childhood in a very different landscape: the enclosed green world of Virginia's Shenandoah Valley. In the small farming community of Back Creek, Virginia, where Willa Cather was born in 1873, men were in charge of the land and the money; women were in charge of the kitchens and the stories. On the surface, this was an unequal distribution of power, common to all patriarchal cultures, and we can see sources here for Cather's male identification during her adolescence and college years. But for a novelist who would later put stories into written language and associate creativity with cooking and gardening, this female legacy was an inspirational one, and Cather eventually honored her female lineage when she created the strong pioneer heroines of her first novels.

Although the Back Creek region was not wealthy, the Cathers were among its most prominent citizens. Willa Cather's great-grandfather, James Cather, was a successful farmer and stock-raiser. His son William Cather—Willa's grandfather—followed his father's example by establishing a thriving sheep farm and building the comfortable house Willow Shade, where Willa was born.

In 1877, William decided to resettle on the Nebraska frontier. His son George had already emigrated there, and letters home reported that the soil was richer than Virginia's, and the climate more healthful. So William and his wife, Caroline, left Virginia, never to return. Six years later, Willa's father, Charles, would decide to join his parents and brother, and the family headed westward.

Charles Cather was less the hardworking, entrepreneurial farmer than his forebears had been: gentle, thoughtful, well-read, he was not really suited to farming. When the family moved to Nebraska, he ultimately found more congenial work in a real estate and loan office in Red Cloud, a small prairie town.

A self-educated man who enjoyed reading poetry aloud to his children, Charles Cather supported Willa's desire to attend college, although he never fully understood the urgency of her drive to become a great artist. But when fellow novelist Sinclair Lewis told an Omaha audience in 1920 that he considered Willa Cather "Nebraska's foremost citizen," her father wrote her a loving, congratulatory letter: he was proud of his famous literary daughter. Willa returned the tribute when she reissued her collection of poetry *April Twilights* in 1923 and dedicated it "to my Father for a Valentine."

Willa's relationship with her gentlemanly father was close and untroubled. He became one source for a recurring figure in her fiction: the sensitive, aesthetic man of integrity who is never at ease in a callous, materialistic world. Such male characters include Carl Linstrum in *O Pioneers!* and Tom Outland in *The Professor's House* as well as those based

FROM VIRGINIA TO NEBRASKA

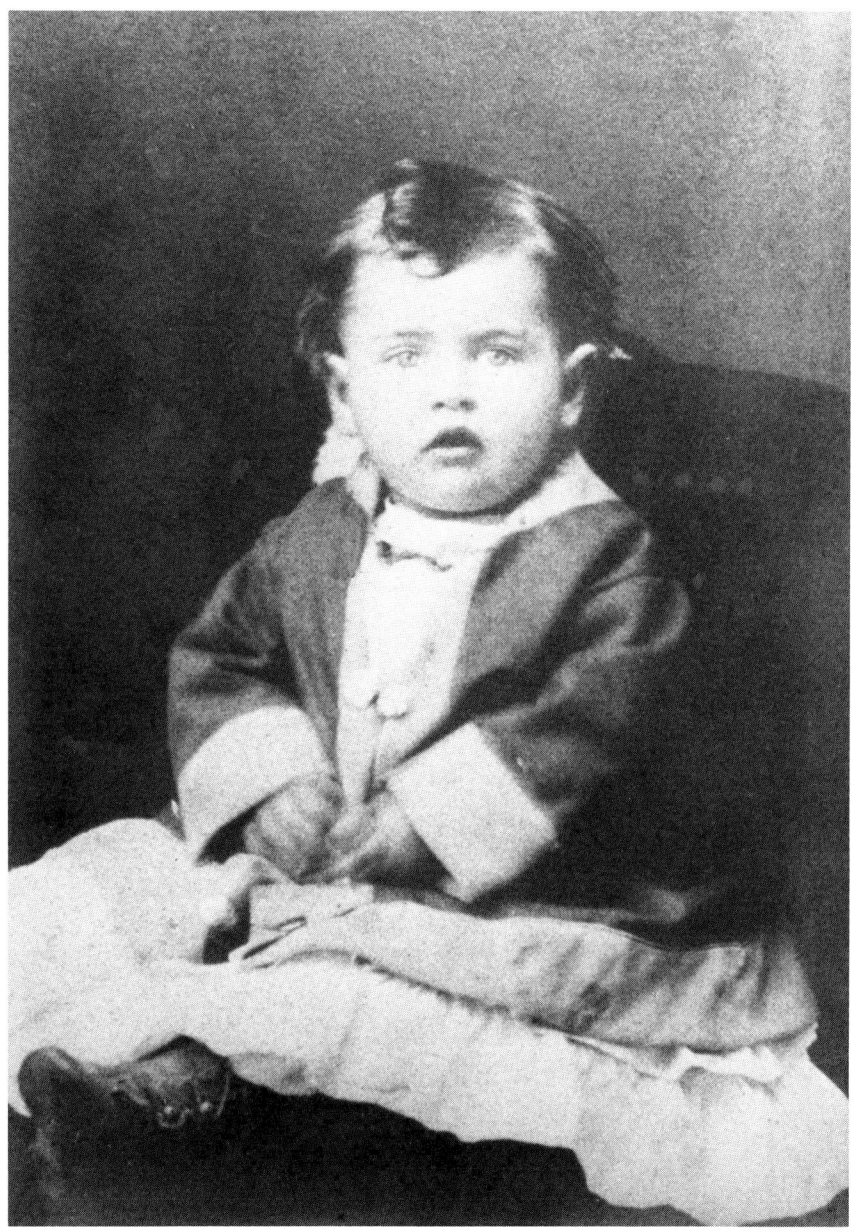

Cather as a baby in Virginia. Despite her delicate attire, Willa was rebellious and outspoken at an early age, defying what she later called the "smooth, unreal conventions about little girls."

WILLA CATHER

Willa's father, Charles Fectigue Cather, was a sensitive, well-read man who was hardworking and successful but lacked his daughter's driving ambition.

more directly on her father: Euclide Auclair in *Shadows on the Rock* and Hillary Templeton in "Old Mrs. Harris," perhaps Cather's most autobiographical story.

Like many daughters, Cather had a far more intense, conflict-ridden, and passionate bond with her mother than she did with her father. When the author entered her forties and finally claimed her creative power with *O Pioneers!* she would find the mother-daughter bond a source of great imaginative strength, and powerful mother figures can be found in many of her novels. But she and her mother—both strong-willed women—were bound to clash. Until Willa managed the difficult emotional process of separation and adult reconnection, it was hard for her to make use of the powerful dynamics of the mother-daughter bond in her writing.

Mary Virginia Boak Cather was an attractive, imperious southern lady, not the decorous, submissive wife imagined by Victorian era advice-givers. Proud of her beauty and appearance, she was known for changing her outfits several times a day and never emerged from her bedroom until her long hair was beautifully arranged. It was as if being a lady was an act, and Virginia Cather did not like people to catch her backstage. In later years, when her daughter wanted to please her with a gift, Willa would choose jewelry, perfume, delicate lingerie—all tributes to her mother's feminine beauty.

Virginia Cather was a woman of contradictions: this clothes-conscious beauty was also the family disciplinarian, subduing unruly children with a rawhide whip. "Her will was law," stated Edith Lewis, who shared a New York apartment with Cather for almost 40 years and wrote a memoir of their shared life. "To show [Virginia Cather] disrespect was an unthinkable offense," Lewis continued, "and her displeasure was more dreaded than any other catastrophe that could happen." And yet Willa's mother was also thoughtful, considerate, and sympathetic. In Lewis's opinion, it took Willa years to understand her mother's volatile, paradoxical nature—"quick to resent, quick to sympathize, headstrong, passionate, and yet capable of great kindness and understanding."

Virginia Cather's regal nature was contradicted by her many illnesses, some related to pregnancy and childbirth. Willa was her firstborn, and she would have seven children in all: Roscoe, Douglass, and Jessica were born in Virginia; James, Elsie, and John in Nebraska. Doctors were frequently in attendance at the Cather home, and like many Victorian women, Virginia Cather may have found release from onerous family responsibilities—as well as attention—when she took on the invalid's role.

WILLA CATHER

In later years, Edith Lewis recalled, Willa Cather "always said she was more like her mother than any other member of her family," and indeed both women were dominating figures, despite their different destinies. Yet before Cather could acknowledge these similarities, like other daughters she strove to establish difference from her mother. Although her defiance reached a peak during her William Cather period—a flagrant repudiation of her mother's role—it began during her Virginia childhood, when she rejected the role of the southern lady her mother wanted her to play.

Willa Cather liked to tell the story of an early skirmish with her mother that happened at Willow Shade when she was five or six years old. One day, an elderly judge, whom her mother wanted to impress, was visiting. He began to stroke Willa's curls, complementing her on being such a nice, well-behaved little girl. Then Willa suddenly horrified her mother when she burst out of her "nice girl" role and told the judge she was a "dang'ous nigger"—hardly an identity that would win the heart of a southern judge shortly after the South had lost the Civil War. On the surface, Willa was defying the judge; but the person "horrified" in her memory was her mother—the person who wanted her daughter to be polite and feminine, and the real object of the daughter's attack. Even as a young child, Willa found the conventions of the southern lady confining, and she refused to be imprisoned by her mother's—and her society's—expectations for female behavior.

Although she was a bright, attractive, and at times imperious woman, Virginia Cather was still limited by the constraints of the feminine role. She wanted to be polite to judges in her parlor, and she wanted her daughter to do the same. Her fierce energies could find no outlet in the public world: after she had married and become a mother, her choices were limited. When her husband decided to emigrate to Nebraska and join his own relatives, for example, Virginia Cather had no choice but to accompany him, leaving her childhood home, her friends, and her relatives for a raw new environment where she felt displaced and diminished.

In her last novel, *Sapphira and the Slave Girl,* Willa Cather created a character who reflects her mother's contradictory combination of

FROM VIRGINIA TO NEBRASKA

Willa's mother, Mary Virginia Boak Cather, was a woman with strong southern roots, and she found the Cather family's move from Virginia to Nebraska in 1883 extremely difficult. Twelve years later, she wrote to a friend that she still longed for Virginia's "familiar earth."

power and powerlessness. Sapphira Colbert, perhaps the most ambiguous mother figure in Cather's fiction, is an outrageous, bright, controlling woman confined to a wheelchair. Because she is crippled, Cather suggests, Sapphira's desire for power takes darker, more subterranean and manipulative routes than it would have had she been granted more authority by her culture. The metaphor of the wheelchair suggests that in some ways Cather felt her mother's power had been crippled or weakened and distorted because she did not possess a role in which she could express her imagination and vitality. In a sense, when she followed a career in the public world as a journalist and novelist, Willa was living out her mother's unlived ambitions—expressing a part of her mother's self that never found a voice.

Willa Cather's grandmothers—Caroline Cather and Rachel Boak—found more harmonious expressions of their power in the farmwife's traditional role. The fictional characters Cather based on them do not display the conflicts she saw in her own mother. When her husband, William, decided to emigrate from Virginia to Nebraska, Caroline accompanied him uncomplainingly as a dutiful wife should and threw herself into her domestic work with fortitude and endurance—gardening, cooking, canning, preserving. Her letters are filled with references to religion and work, and evidently she could command male family members if woman's work required it: "I got my garden made last Tuesday," she wrote to a daughter back in Virginia—"Uncle John don the work and I don the bossing." But in her marriage to William, Caroline knew she could not do the bossing. Authority lay with her husband, and if they ever had a difference of opinion she knew it was the wife's place to yield.

Drawing on her memories of Caroline Cather in creating Grandmother Burden in *My Ántonia,* Cather describes a "strong woman, of unusual endurance," who survives uprooting by quickly establishing woman's traditional domains: she plants a garden and fashions a homey, warm kitchen decorated with curtains, flowers, and plants. In this maternal realm, her grandson Jim Burden—the novel's narrator—feels safe and protected, as if in a "tight, warm boat" on a winter sea.

Rachel Seibert Boak, Cather's maternal grandmother, received the most affectionate portrait of a family member we can find in Cather's fiction—the loving, self-denying grandmother in "Old Mrs. Harris" who does everything she can to see her granddaughter attend college. Rachel Boak was a more important emotional presence in her granddaughter's life than Caroline Cather: she lived with the family in both

Virginia and Nebraska and was like a second mother to Willa. She read aloud to her granddaughter and taught her to read and write, so from the first Willa had reason to associate language with a female presence. In "Old Mrs. Harris," Cather delicately suggests the legacy connecting grandmother and granddaughter by portraying Mrs. Harris as a woman who "loved to read, anything at all, the Bible or the continued story in the Chicago weekly paper," a fitting ancestor for a granddaughter who wants to attend a university and enter the public world of books and reading.

Outside the family, Cather encountered other women who could be models for a woman writer—women storytellers, women who naturally possessed the gifts of an oral culture. She later said her first introduction to narrative was meeting women who came down from the mountains to help out at Willow Shade with "spinning and quilting, butter-making and preserving and candle-making." The young Willa would hide under the quilting frames and listen to the folklore, gossip, and legends the women passed around while they sewed. Mary Ann Anderson, model for Mrs. Ringer in *Sapphira and the Slave Girl,* was the premier storyteller, and when Cather was older she would listen to her for hours. It was worth being sick as a child, Cather remembered later, because she would get a visit and a story from Mrs. Anderson.

Although none of the women quilters would have thought of their work as art or their conversation as storytelling, today we can see the connections between quilting and narrative. Quilting itself was a collective act of creativity, with a group of women connecting pieces of fabric into a larger and harmonious whole, just as their stories wove together the history of their community with that of their listeners. Frequently, quilts became stories themselves, as women recorded important family events among their patterns—births, marriages, deaths—and passed these heirlooms on to their daughters, a kind of diary or family history crafted from their domestic skills. When Cather became a writer of fiction, she reworked and retold some of the stories she had heard. Her fiction itself sometimes resembles patchwork—novels such as *My Ántonia* and *Death Comes for the Archbishop* weave together a series of smaller stories, just the way a quilt connects pieces of fabric. As a novelist whose written, published stories reached the reading public, Cather could give her stories both the permanence and the audience the farm women could not attain with their quilts and conversations.

So although the women Willa Cather knew in her Virginia childhood followed the traditional female role, they were strong, resourceful, and creative people. Her mother, her female relatives, the farm women in Virginia and Nebraska—all these women in different ways defied the Victorian notion that women were the inferior sex, weak and yielding. And Willa Cather's mother may have given her the greatest gift of all: even though she may not always have approved of her daughter's defiance, she always gave her the freedom to be herself, and so Willa Cather could move into adulthood knowing that self-expression was not inconsistent with being a valued daughter.

In 1883, the sheep barn at Willow Shade burned down, and Charles Cather decided to join his parents and brother George in Webster Country, Nebraska, located on the Divide—the plains between the Republican and the Little Blue rivers. The Cather family could travel all the way from Back Creek to Red Cloud by train, but once they left the town for William and Caroline Cather's farmhouse, where they would stay for more than a year, signs of civilization vanished. Willa Cather was thrown into the unsettled landscape she describes in *My Ántonia,* when her narrator, Jim Burden, enters a seemingly empty realm he can only define in negatives: "There seemed to be nothing to see; no fences, no creeks or trees, no hills or fields. If there was a road, I could not make it out in the faint starlight. There was nothing but land: not a country at all, but the material out of which countries are made. No, there was nothing but land . . ."

Like Jim Burden, until she saw the Nebraska prairies, Willa Cather had never before "looked up at the sky when there was not a familiar mountain ridge against it." The topography of Virginia, where a line of hills surrounded Back Creek Valley, was sheltered and embracing; that of Nebraska, where undulating treeless plains stretched out in every direction toward the horizon, was open and exposed. In Nebraska, as in all flat lands, the sky seemed vaster than in Virginia, where trees and mountain ridges rose up against it.

FROM VIRGINIA TO NEBRASKA

For Cather, as for many people who move from a sheltered to an open landscape, the move had strong emotional resonance. Not only was she being transplanted—difficult for children, who generally resist change—but she was being moved into an unprotected landscape where she experienced a "kind of erasure of personality." She felt as if she did not really exist in this new country, for the drastic change in landscape unsettled her supposedly stable sense of identity.

"I would not know," Cather said later, "how much a child's life is bound up in the woods and hills and meadows around it, if I had not been jerked away from all these and thrown out into a country as bare as a piece of sheet iron. I had heard from my father you had to show grit in a new country . . . but . . . I thought I should go under." She added, "For the first week or two on the homestead I had that kind of contraction of the stomach which comes from homesickness. I didn't like canned things anyhow, and I made an agreement with myself that I would not eat much until I got back to Virginia and could get some fresh mutton."

Later, Cather told a friend she had almost died from homesickness during the first year in Nebraska. She had left a beautiful environment for an ugly, desolate one, she felt during that year, and she did not think she could survive the loss.

But Willa Cather did survive and eventually flourished in her new environment. Nebraska became familiar, became home. In the prairies' openness she found freedom: the break with her past held out the possibility of independence and renewal. She rode horseback across the prairies and learned to love their wide expanses. This love lasted her lifetime. "When I strike the open plains, I'm home," she would say. "That love of great spaces, of rolling open country like the sea—it's the grand passion of my life."

But the young Cather found more than open spaces as she roamed the prairies: she found a world inhabited by people from different countries and cultures who enriched her imagination. In a sense, foreign countries were only miles away, for European settlers "spread across our bronze prairies like the daubs of color on a painter's palette," she said later, bringing vitality and shading to a "neutral new world." "On

A postcard of downtown Red Cloud, Nebraska, shows the small town's residents turning out to watch a convoy of automobiles.

Sunday we could drive to a Norwegian church and listen to a sermon in that language," Cather recalled, "or to a Danish or Swedish church. We could go to the French Catholic settlement in the next county . . . or we could go to church with the German Lutherans."

She particularly liked to visit the immigrant farm women, who became important replacements for the storytellers of Willow Shade. She would spend hours in their kitchens, listening to their talk and eating their cooking: "I must eat a great deal and enjoy it," she said later, and evidently she had no trouble pleasing them. They, in turn, gave the uprooted child maternal warmth. "They understood my homesickness and were kind to me," Cather remembered.

In their halting English, these women would tell Willa stories about the homes, traditions, and customs they had left behind in Europe. Doubtless, Cather found consolation in their stories of loss and re-settlement because she, too, had left her own country behind her. She loved their stories. "They talked more freely to a child than to grown people," she said, "and I always felt as if every word they said to me counted for twenty." After spending a morning with a pioneer woman who was baking bread or making butter, she would "ride home in the most unreasonable state of excitement," she remembered, "as if they told me so much more than they said—as if I had got inside another person's skin."

Later, Cather attributed her desire to write fiction to her conversations with these neighbors. "The stories used to go round and round in my head at night. This was, for me, the initial impulse. I didn't know any writing people. I had an enthusiasm for a kind of country and a kind of people, rather than ambition."

Throughout her life, Cather remained sensitive to the processes of uprooting, transplantation, and resettlement: the move to Nebraska stamped her creative imagination forever. Time and again, her novelist's imagination was drawn to individuals and groups who leave one home for another: a slave girl who escapes to Canada; a professor who finds himself unable to leave his old house; the immigrants who settled the Nebraska Divide; the French settlers in 17th-century Quebec; the Spanish and French missionaries in the American Southwest; the Native Americans who migrated to the Southwest and built their homes into the cliffs of Arizona and New Mexico. When she wrote these stories in her fiction, she was concerned not with simple survival during the process of transplantation but with the capability of human beings to find spiritual and emotional meaning in their new landscapes—the capability to make the strange become familiar and to make houses become homes.

The Cather family moved to Red Cloud in 1884. According to local newspapers, the family wanted to be closer to schools and doctors; but Virginia Cather also found the isolation of farming life uncongenial. Charles Cather opened a real estate and loan office, and the family moved into a frame house close to the center of town. In contrast to Willow Shade, the house was small and cramped, and later Cather could speak with authority of the struggle to keep hold of her "individual soul" in the midst of the "general family flavour." Eventually, her mother—sensitive to her adolescent daughter's need for privacy—had an ell-shaped wing partitioned from the main attic as a bedroom for Willa, who soon grew to love having her own space. In the autobiographical first section of her 1915 novel *The Song of the Lark,* Cather's alter ego Thea Kronborg finds the acquisition of her attic bedroom "one of the most important things that ever happened to her." Until then, surrounded by a large and growing family, Thea felt her inner voice "drowned" by the tumult around her; but in her attic room, she begins to discover her own voice and self.

During her years in Red Cloud, Cather found happy companionship as well as enriching solitude. She was close to her two brothers Roscoe and Douglass, and they spent many hours exploring the Republican River and its sandbars. She formed close friendships with the Miner girls: Mary, Irene, Margie, and Carrie, the daughters of neighbors. She and the Miners acted together in amateur theatricals and created imaginative games, such as their construction of a whole town named Sandy Point from crates and packing boxes, dominating the Cathers' backyard. Not surprisingly, Willa was mayor. She maintained her friendship with the Miners all her life.

Like Thea in *The Song of the Lark,* Cather enjoyed several adult "friends of childhood" who gave her guidance and encouragement. Two female teachers, Mrs. Goudy and Miss King, were her supporters and allies. She also found an informal teacher in Will Ducker, a local druggist who tutored her in Greek and Latin as well as science. After her interest in medicine was sparked, Willa found the town's two physicians, Dr. McKeeby and Dr. Damerell, helpful mentors. Dr. Damerell took her on as an informal apprentice, once allowing her to administer chloroform to a patient before he performed an operation. "How I loved the long rambling buggy rides we used to take," Cather reminisced later. "I could tell who lived at every place and about the ailments of his family. The old country doctor and I used to talk over his cases. I was determined then to be a surgeon."

Cather's fascination with surgery may have been one source for her William Cather impersonation; certainly, her "William Cather, M.D." signature reflected her identification with her medical mentors. She also

FROM VIRGINIA TO NEBRASKA

pursued her medical studies independently. After setting up a makeshift laboratory in her basement, she began dissecting toads and frogs. These practices made her the subject of disapproving gossip, but she persisted. Her unorthodox hobbies dominate the entries she made in a friend's album book in 1888. In recording her likes and dislikes, Cather termed

Roscoe and Douglass Cather, two of Willa's six younger siblings. Roscoe, Douglass, Willa, and other children in the neighborhood spent many hours exploring neighboring rivers and staging theatricals.

her idea of perfect happiness to be "Amputating limbs," and her favorite summer pastime "Slicing Toads." Her all-around favorite amusement was "Vivisection," her chief goal in life "To be an M.D."

Cather's desire to be a doctor is understandable—this was a profession imbued with power. Of course, all professional roles in the 19th century were associated with men; but Cather's desire to be a doctor was a particularly strong repudiation of conventional gender roles, because the male doctor/female patient pairing mirrored the society's definition of strength as masculine and weakness as feminine. Her drive to "be an M.D." also shows the daughter's desire to declare her difference from her mother—Cather wanted to be the powerful rescuer, not the helpless female invalid. This pattern continued throughout her life. She liked to be in control of people, events, and herself, and thus found her own illnesses very difficult to bear: the invalid's loss of control placed her back in the dependent female role she had repudiated along with Victorian definitions of true womanhood.

In *My Ántonia,* Cather evokes the narrow, constricting aspects of small-town life—the small-mindedness, the conservatism, the fear of difference. Certainly, she experienced these negative qualities in Red Cloud: small towns offer community, but they can also try to police their members through criticism and gossip. Indeed, Jim Burden credits the "tongue of gossip" with keeping Red Cloud youth in line, ensuring that the young men will not follow the sensuous, working-class "hired girls" but will marry the respectable middle-class girls who attend the same church. The object of gossip herself during her adolescence, Cather knew what it was like to be talked about by people with narrower values than her own.

But in Red Cloud, Cather was not simply the object of gossip; as on the Divide, she became the inheritor of stories that eventually shaped her fiction. The first story she heard in Nebraska was about the death of Annie Sadilek's father by suicide; Cather later reworked the event in her first short story, "Peter," and then again as the death of Mr. Shimerda in *My Ántonia.* Many of the people whose lives touched hers in Red Cloud eventually became transformed into characters in her fiction, as Annie Sadilek was the inspiration for Ántonia, and Mrs.

FROM VIRGINIA TO NEBRASKA

Cather's attic room in her home in Red Cloud, Nebraska. Having a quiet space where she could work proved essential to Cather's success as a writer.

Silas Garber, the wife of Nebraska's governor, the model for Marian Forrester in *A Lost Lady*. Thus, the town, as well as the country, gave Cather rich soil from which her fiction would grow.

Willa Cather once described Nebraska as a "highway for dreamers and adventurers." Certainly, it was for her. Virginia had its writers and historians, but Nebraska was open land for the pen as well as the plow. "Except for some of the people who lived in it," Edith Lewis wrote, "I think no one had ever found Nebraska beautiful until Willa Cather wrote about it." It would take Cather years before she turned her gaze back to Nebraska; but when she did, she found a storehouse of literary material that would last her a lifetime.

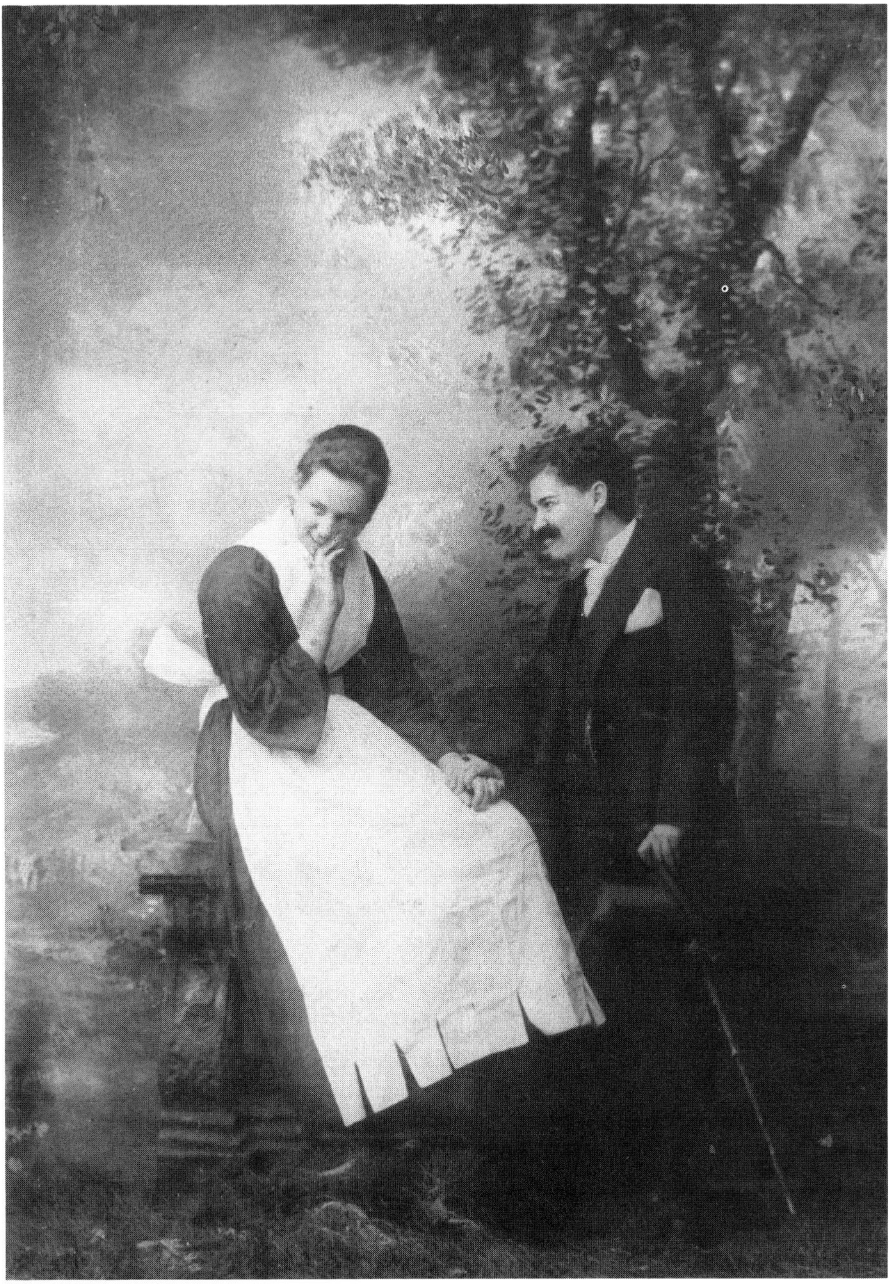

CHAPTER THREE

"THE THING NOT NAMED"

In 1890, Willa Cather became the first person in her family to attend college when she left Red Cloud for the University of Nebraska at Lincoln. At that time, higher education was generally thought to be wasted on daughters, whose task in life was to marry and have children; few women attended college. But the University of Nebraska—like the University of Michigan, the University of Wisconsin, and the other large midwestern land-grant institutions founded during the 1870s and 1880s—was coeducational from the start, and Cather's parents supported her desire to attend the local university. (Had the family stayed in Virginia, she would have been less fortunate: the University of Virginia did not admit women until the 1970s.)

Like other students, Cather found a room for herself in a local boardinghouse and threw herself into the scholar's life, determined to succeed. She enrolled in the university's preparatory school in 1890; as a gradu-

Cather (right) poses in 1894 for a promotional photo for a University of Nebraska theatrical production.

ate of an untried small high school, she required a year of additional work before matriculating as a freshman in 1891. At first, she still intended to be a doctor, and she took science courses and signed some letters home "William Cather, M.D." But she followed up her strong interest in the classics, begun under Will Ducker's tutelage, and decorated her room—as would Jim Burden in *My Ántonia*—with a map of Rome. By the spring of 1891, she had transferred her enthusiasm from science to literature and began experimenting with writing fiction.

In describing Thea Kronborg's departure from her Colorado home for Chicago in *The Song of the Lark,* Cather gives her eastbound heroine a sense of completeness and self-sufficiency: "Everything that was essential seemed to be right there in the car with her. She lacked nothing." But at 16, Willa Cather was not as confident as she later imagined Thea to be. As a country-educated student entering university, Cather sensed, as her friend Edith Lewis observed, a "whole continent of ignorance surrounding her in every direction, like the flat land itself; separating her from everything she admired, everything she longed for and wanted to become." Years later, when Cather was traveling in sophisticated Boston and New York literary circles, she could still feel insecure because of her prairie background and the gaps in her knowledge—embarrassed, for example, when a Boston hostess whom Cather admired discovered that she did not know John Donne's poetry.

During her years at the University of Nebraska, Cather devoured American, English, Continental, and classical literature. She did well in her studies and was thought brilliant by her classmates. Yet as she became increasingly familiar with the Western literary tradition, learning to admire writers such as William Shakespeare, Thomas Carlyle, and Gustave Flaubert and beginning to write short fiction herself, she still felt a sense of exclusion from the culture she wanted to inherit.

Cather had many reasons for sensing herself a cultural outsider. As a woman, she was separated by gender from the authors of most of the works she admired; as an American, she suffered from the same sense of inferiority vis-à-vis European culture that bothered male writers such

"THE THING NOT NAMED"

Although Cather's habit of dressing as a man caused more furor, she could be equally flamboyant when wearing traditional women's clothing. She favored opulent formal attire, as in this 1895 photo taken before her graduation ball.

as Henry James and T. S. Eliot; as a middle-class Nebraskan, she lacked an inherited sense of cultural privilege that upper-class New Englanders could enjoy. And lastly, during her years at the University of Nebraska, Cather fell in love with a woman, a fellow student named Louise Pound, and began to confront what we would now call her lesbian identity. Sensing that her attraction to intense female friendships was deemed

WILLA CATHER

"unnatural" by her society, Cather had another reason for feeling different from her colleagues.

Feeling all these various kinds of exclusion or marginality, Cather, who was shifting her allegiance from medicine to literature, doubted that she could ever be a great writer. Surely, this was too much to aspire to. She could be a critic perhaps, or a newspaperwoman, and maybe even write a few short stories that would appear in college publications. But join the ranks of Virgil and Shakespeare, or even of Rudyard Kipling and Robert Louis Stevenson? How was this possible? And looking back, where were the great women writers? There were a few women writers she could admire—George Eliot, Jane Austen, George Sand, Charlotte Brontë, and, further back, the Greek lesbian poet Sappho—but the great literary tradition she studied and admired in university was overwhelmingly male. She did not have what we would now call models, and so it was hard for her to imagine that the identities of woman and writer could be reconciled.

But the role of an outsider, although painful during one's early years, can be a useful one for a writer who needs to feel some separation or difference from the dominant culture in the struggle to find an individual voice. And people who feel themselves outsiders can be sharp observers and evaluators of their fellow human beings—traits that can sharpen the novelist's eye for detail.

So Willa Cather's sense of difference also gave her a sense of specialness, and indeed many of her Nebraska classmates remembered her as arrogant and opinionated. Unlike many of her classmates, she was not going to return to a small town in Nebraska and take up farming, or banking, or motherhood.

Willa Cather associated her William Cather persona with power, autonomy, and achievement, so she brought this persona with her from Red Cloud to manage the difficult, and probably frightening, transition to Lincoln. A classmate described other students' uneasy laughter when confronted with Cather's disturbingly androgynous figure: "While the students were sitting in the classroom waiting for the instructor to arrive, the door opened and a head appeared with short hair and a straw hat. A masculine voice inquired if this were the beginning Greek class, and when someone said it was, the body attached to the head and hat opened the door wider and came in. The masculine head and voice were attached to a girl's body and skirts. The entire class laughed, but Willa Cather, apparently unperturbed, took her seat and joined the waiting students."

In 1948, Cather's Nebraska classmates were asked to record their memories of their famous colleague. Almost every respondent mentioned her rejection of traditional feminine dress and manners. "She was the first girl that I ever saw in suspenders," wrote one. Others mentioned her "dark man-tailored suits" and her "mannish-cut dress"—the shirtwaist popular among the "New Women" of the 1890s, who were challenging Victorian stereotypes in feminine behavior and dress.

Cather's classmates did not view her as masculine solely because of her dress. They mentioned many personality traits that Victorian culture—and to some extent our culture now—would define as masculine rather than as broadly human: words such as "assertive," "energetic," "outspoken," "individualistic," "independent," "forceful," "strong," "self-confident," and "brilliant" are sprinkled through their recollections of Cather's college years. These traits, most concluded, were simply not feminine. Cather just did not like "girls' ways or manners," observed one classmate.

Although Cather attracted disapproval or laughter from some classmates, she stuck to her own course, refusing to sacrifice parts of herself in order to be accepted. She was not yet a writer, but she was preserving the independence of mind and soul that would allow her to become one.

During her college years, Cather made some changes in her clothes and dress, becoming less mannish. As she became surer of who she was, she felt freer to experiment and to try on different identities. Two photographs taken in 1895, her senior year, show this transition. In one, her hair—now long—is carefully arranged for a trip to the opera, and she appears elegant, perhaps even overdressed, in a Persian lamb cloak and a very fashionable ostrich plume hat. In the other photograph, she is dressed for her graduation ball in an ivory satin gown trimmed with gold sequins.

WILLA CATHER

In her adult years, Cather would enjoy a wide, eclectic, and personal taste in dress: at times preferring expensive, tasteful, and on occasion regal feminine attire; at other times opting for casual or outdoor clothes. But she would always dress to suit herself and the occasion—she did not have to use costume to make statements about gender. This process began at the University of Nebraska, where Cather began to sense that the power and creativity she wanted did not inhere in a mannish suit or a short haircut but were qualities that were increasingly emerging from within her. As she took more risks and began to discover her own powers, she did not need a male persona to signify her difference from the conventional female destiny.

Throughout her college years, Cather found Lincoln a congenial environment: this was an intellectual community where people cared about and fervently discussed ideas. The central student organizations were the debating and literary societies, where students presented papers and argued the merits of poets, artists, and writers. It is hard to imagine that at many universities today a student could follow Willa Cather's route to college fame: impressed by her essay on British prose writer Thomas Carlyle, one of her professors had it printed in the local newspaper. A short time later, everyone was talking about it.

Cather soon became involved with several campus publications. Along with Louise Pound, she edited the *Lasso,* a literary magazine; she became managing editor of the campus magazine the *Hesperian,* the only woman on the editorial staff; and later, she was literary editor of the yearbook. Cather also joined the university's literary and debating societies, where she gained a reputation for articulate attacks or "roasting." She continued her flair for drama—and for adopting male roles—by taking part in college theatricals.

After Cather had established her reputation as a student and a college journalist, she took more and more time away from her studies during her last two years, when she began writing for the Lincoln newspapers, reviewing plays, and writing columns on the arts. One observer of the local media thought Cather was at the "head of the Lincoln writers." She was never one to be timid in expressing her opinions, and she was known for her cutting, slashing style of writing. Cather liked to "roast" inept actors or shabby theatrical companies and was referred to by some as that "meat-ax young girl" who could rip apart a play or a performance with a few well-chosen barbs.

As in Red Cloud, Cather was helped both in school and in her newspaper work by male mentors who recognized her talent and encouraged her. Two faculty members in the English department urged her to write essays and short stories: Charles Gere, publisher of the Lincoln *Journal* and father of her good friend Mariel Gere, supervised her newspaper career, along with managing editor Will Owen Jones; and the drama critic for the *Evening News,* another Lincoln paper, helped her learn the reviewer's craft.

Cather received more support for her professional goals than did many aspiring women writers in the 19th century. (Edith Wharton, for example, had a much lonelier road to follow to discover her literary talents.) As a journalist, Cather could develop her writing skills and literary self-confidence in the same training ground that fostered so many male writers of her era and later: Stephen Crane, Theodore Dreiser, and Ernest Hemingway, among others. Even though Lincoln later seemed to her an unsophisticated prairie city in comparison to New York or Boston, the university and the community were kind to her ambitions. Western cities, still imbued with the pioneer spirit of egalitarianism, were sometimes more open to independent women than were eastern ones.

During her college years, Cather did more than devote herself to work, study, and writing: she also devoted herself to friendship. Her classmate Mariel Gere became a lifelong friend, as did Dorothy Canfield, daughter of the university's chancellor, James Canfield. Later, Canfield became a prize-winning novelist and a judge for the Book-of-the-Month Club, and Cather could always discuss literary as well as emotional matters with her. And then there was the bewitching Louise Pound.

Writing to Dorothy Canfield (then Dorothy Canfield Fisher) in 1921, Willa Cather characterized her undergraduate years as a tempestuous era during which she was often overwhelmed by emotional storms. The storm center of the early 1890s was Louise Pound. The two young women were at first drawn together by their shared interest in the arts. They collaborated in the fall of 1891 as associate editors of the *Lasso* and acted together in the drama society. The following year, Cather had a prominent role in *A Perjured Padulion,* a satiric play about university life written by Pound.

Three years ahead of Cather at the university, Pound was the fabled "New Woman" of the 1890s—the decade when the college woman, the sportswoman, and the professional woman began to symbolize female emancipation. Daughter of a prominent Lincoln family, Pound was a talented musician, outstanding athlete, and campus leader. She went on to gain a Ph.D. in English and a distinguished career as a philologist and folklorist, eventually becoming at the age of 82 the first female president of the Modern Language Association. A few months later, she was the first woman elected to the Nebraska Sports Hall of Fame. "First woman again," Pound wrote to a friend after receiving this honor. "Life has its humors."

Although not embittered by the discrimination she encountered during her long career—she kept her sense of humor—Pound was well aware of the injustices professional women often encountered in male-dominated fields. "When a man does well," she said, "it is taken for granted he is typical. When a woman does well (So strong is the tradition), it is still thought to need explanation; and it is taken for granted that she is not typical but is the product of special circumstances."

When Cather first met her, Pound was already accumulating her athletic triumphs. An expert cyclist, skater, tennis player, and golfer, she won medals and titles in several sports. Pound's brother Roscoe claimed his sister could "pitch a good curve ball, could bat, throw and field with the rest of us." Pound managed and captained the women's basketball team and helped to organize a women's military drill company. At times, Pound wore boyish garb, as in one photograph she and Cather had taken together; another photograph, however, shows a more conventionally feminine appearance: a delicate-featured young woman with long hair gracefully swept up in a bun, wearing a dress with fashionable leg-of-mutton sleeves and a gold necklace. Proud of

"THE THING NOT NAMED"

Louise Pound (left) and Cather sport their notorious boyish garb. Cather found the accomplished and flamboyant Pound fascinating, but their friendship soon soured, perhaps because Pound was put off by the intensity of Cather's feelings.

her red hair, Pound later formed an organization of redheaded women she called the Order of the Golden Fleece.

Willa Cather was drawn to Louise Pound because of her intelligence, energy, and accomplishments—this was a woman she could respect. And she was also drawn to her because of her beauty. Pound must have seemed pleasingly, intriguingly contradictory to Cather—combining an attractive feminine appearance with unconventional abilities and interests—and Cather's letters to Pound show her taking the role of the insecure, infatuated lover.

Writing to Pound in 1892, Cather told her how beautiful she had seemed at a party the night before and went on to praise, in detail, Louise's gown. Pound had looked stunning, Cather confided, and she

Dorothy Canfield, pictured here as an undergraduate at the University of Nebraska. Canfield, who met Cather in college and remained a lifelong friend, became the well-known novelist Dorothy Fisher.

enjoyed making a young man who was also admiring her feel jealous. In the rest of the letter, Cather told Louise of her strong feelings—her jealousy of her other friends, her despair that she would not be seeing her over the summer, her surprise that her feelings were so strong. It was unfair that feminine friendship should be unnatural, Cather wrote, but she supposed that it was. She ended the letter asking for Louise's patience with her and signed it "William."

Over a year later, Cather was still romantically preoccupied with Pound. She wrote her a long letter from Red Cloud, asking for proof of her affection and pleading for a visit. She was depressed, Cather admitted, unsure about Louise's love and commitment. Only Louise had the power to dispel her sadness, or to intensify it—could she come to Red Cloud and save her friend from misery and yearning?

Perhaps Pound found Cather's intensity too overwhelming. In any case, a break occurred, and Cather was deeply hurt, as she confided to Mariel Gere. In 1894, Cather published a satiric attack on Louise's

"THE THING NOT NAMED"

brother Roscoe in the student newspaper. It is not clear whether the attack resulted from or accelerated Louise's withdrawal; but after the sketch appeared, there was a sharp rift between Cather and the Pound family. Although Cather occasionally corresponded with Pound in later years, she never rebuilt the friendship.

Relationships with women, both friendships and romantic attachments, would be important to Cather all her life, providing her the intimacy she needed as well as the support for the solitude she required for her work and travel. Cather was not indifferent to men—she had several important male friendships and professional relationships, and was close to her father and brothers. But the bonds with women gave her the nourishment she needed, both as a woman and as a writer.

The complexity and multiplicity of Cather's attachments reveals how impoverished our categories such as *heterosexual* and *homosexual* are to describe human desire, sexuality, and identity. Many people, such as Cather, have close relationships with people of both sexes, and these bonds may be erotic even if sexual desire or attraction is never acknowledged consciously. It is difficult, too, when dealing with a figure from the past, to assess the nature of her friendships and to describe that shimmering, intangible quality of personal identity. From the letters Cather left and from her friends' reminiscences, we know something about the emotional quality of her friendships; but we do not know how, or if, they were sexual. Given her experiences, and the understanding of sexual passion she shows in her fiction, it seems she understood sexual desire very well; but there can be no concrete "proof" of this assertion.

Not all of Cather's biographers and critics regard her as a lesbian. Some view her as celibate or asexual; some do not raise the question of sexual identity or orientation at all. In my view, she was a lesbian, and that identity is important for us to consider because it had a great impact on her fiction, particularly on the creative process. As I explore my reasons for viewing Cather as possessing a lesbian identity, I want to caution us to remember that her sexuality was only one strand in her sense of self. I doubt that she got up every day and said to herself, "All right, Willa Cather, lesbian writer, it is time to get to work." The problem is ours, really: as soon as we apply the category *homosexual* or *lesbian* to someone, that sexual identity may be all we can see. For the person concerned, however, the sense of self is composed of many roles and identities: Willa Cather was a lesbian, and she was also a daughter, an aunt, a Nebraskan, a newspaperwoman, an editor, a friend, a novelist, a sister, a lover of good food and wine, a reader, a traveler, a voter, an American. The reason we need to pay particular attention to Cather's lesbianism and its impact on her creativity is that none of these other identities are condemned by our dominant culture as deviant.

Before we can even speak about Cather as a lesbian, however, I need to define how I am using the term. The meaning of *lesbian* is not self-evident and in recent years has been much debated. Actually, genital sexual experience with women has been the least-used criterion. As several critics have observed, to adopt a narrow sexual definition requires the unearthing of "proof" we do not think necessary in defining writers as heterosexual—proof, moreover, that is usually unavailable, as is the case with Willa Cather. And to define lesbianism in narrowly sexual terms ignores the possibility that a woman who never consciously experienced or acted on sexual desire for another woman might possess a lesbian identity more broadly construed, for example, to include primary emotional bonding with women. The poet Adrienne Rich takes this latter approach in her concept of the "lesbian continuum," which she defines as a "range—through each woman's life and throughout history—of woman-identified experience; not simply the fact that a woman has had or consciously desired genital experience with another woman."

For me, Rich's definition is too all-inclusive. Particularly when we are dealing with a historical figure and a writer, the question for me is whether or not the person self-consciously possessed a lesbian identity, which requires that the concept of lesbianism be present in her cultural environment. Willa Cather's letters to Louise Pound are what demonstrate her lesbian identity according to the definition I am using. When she confessed to Louise that she thought it unfair that feminine friendships were "unnatural," she used a loaded word which reveals that certain intense female friendships were being defined as deviant—

"THE THING NOT NAMED"

Despite Cather's worries about her feelings for Louise Pound, she never expressed the concern that her stereotypically masculine traits were "unnatural." This may be because she viewed gender identity as a role to be played—much like the theatrical role she was playing when this picture was taken.

as lesbian—by the dominant culture. In the 1890s, *unnatural* was a code word, or a euphemism, that meant "deviant," "aberrant," or "homosexual."

Earlier in the 19th century, romantic friendships between women and even lifelong partnerships—the so-called Boston marriages—were quite common and were not categorized as unnatural. During the 1870s and 1880s, and in some cases later, college women developed romantic

WILLA CATHER

"A woman has only one gift and out of the wealth of that one thing she must sing and move with song," Cather observed in 1895. "A woman can be great only in proportion as God put feeling in her."

crushes on each other, a phenomenon known as "smashing"—and they could do this without fearing that their infatuations were unnatural. Women's romantic friendships were thought to be uplifting, even spiritual, and because 19th-century ideology viewed women as passionless, Victorian Americans did not have to assume that sexual desire was part of romantic female friendship.

A woman writer who came of age in this more innocent era would have seen nothing amiss in women's passionate friendships; nor would her readers. So Sarah Orne Jewett, the Maine writer who became

"THE THING NOT NAMED"

Cather's literary mentor, could live in a devoted marriagelike relationship with Annie Fields and was free to make female friendship the dominant subject of her fiction. Born 30 years later than Jewett, Cather used the word *unnatural* to speak about her friendship to Pound, and although friendships with women were central to her life, she almost never wrote about them in her fiction, portraying all intense bonds as heterosexual or as friendships between men. Why the difference?

What historians tell us is that during the last decades of the 19th century, the concept of lesbianism emerged in the medical literature and to some extent in individual consciousnesses. The female world of loving friendship in which Jewett and Fields established their Boston marriage was crumbling by the 1890s, now viewed by historians as "a crucial transitional period" in both the United States and Great Britain, when homosexual identity and practice became part of public awareness. (Some women in this transitional period, however, could still hold onto the earlier notion of acceptable romantic friendship, as historian Lillian Faderman observes.) During the period when Willa Cather was developing her bond with Louise Pound, intense female friendships were being discouraged and lesbianism condemned.

In 1895, Ruth Ashmore, a popular writer whose columns in the *Ladies' Home Journal* Cather read, warned female readers against forming romantic bonds with other young women, as Cather had with Pound. "I like a girl to have many girl-friends; I do not like her to have a girl-sweetheart," Ashmore cautioned, making a distinction that would not have occurred earlier in the century. Such infatuations might have disastrous long-term effects, Ashmore hinted, for a girl who squandered her love on other girls might not have enough left for "Prince Charming when he comes to claim his bride."

Although Cather was not responding directly to Ruth Ashmore, she had internalized a social voice like Ashmore's when she used the word *unnatural* to speak about her feelings for Pound. And yet this voice never crippled or intimidated Cather: certainly, it never persuaded her to wait for Prince Charming. Evidently, she managed, if not to quiet it, to make it only one voice in a conversation. Cather continued to form romantic attachments with women, and she led a flourishing personal and

WILLA CATHER

professional life. After she began publishing fiction, in fact, her novels followed, one after the other, in a steady creative stream.

How did Cather's lesbianism affect her writing? Because she could not write directly of the love relationships that were central to her life, we might assume that her novels were impoverished and she constricted as a writer. How much "better" a novelist she could have been, we might assume, had she been born in a more enlightened era and so been able, like lesbian writers today, to describe lesbian relationships in her fiction.

But this view is too simple and not, I think, accurate. After all, a writer such as E. M. Forster, who concealed his homosexual identity in such novels as *Howards End* and *A Passage to India,* produced great art. When he wrote directly of homosexual desire in the novel *Maurice,* which was never published during his lifetime, in many critics' views he did not equal the craft and power of his "closeted" novels.

Cather herself thought that the creative process involved both "disclosure" and "concealment," and in her 1936 essay "The Novel Demeuble," she argued that the "inexpressible presence of the thing not named" gave fiction its power. On the surface, she was referring to the ways in which fiction is enriched by what is left out, or by experiences and emotions too intangible to be put into words; but, of course, the phrase also suggests the lesbianism that she could not name directly. Yet precisely because she could not write directly of love between women, Cather's imagination was challenged to transform that experience into other contexts—perhaps a mother-daughter relationship, or a bond between two men, or a sexually charged description of landscape. And all these descriptions would have been enriched by the emotions she was not naming directly, just as in *O Pioneers!* Alexandra Bergson's fields are nourished by the "underground river" of her unconscious emotional life.

Some readers of Cather's fiction who concentrate on her need to conceal lesbianism view her as writing heterosexual "cover" stories that hide the subversive homosexual "subtext," which is supposedly the real story that Cather would have written in another social climate, and presumably the story that she wanted to write. So, for example, such a

"THE THING NOT NAMED"

reader might say of *My Ántonia* that the narrator, Jim Burden, is only a mask for a female consciousness, and he is unable to develop or express his love for Ántonia because he is really a stand-in for the lesbian author—in short, a closeted lesbian. Such a reading imagines that the hidden, or encoded, lesbian story is the real one, and the heterosexual plot a surface diversion or camouflage.

My view differs. Certainly, camouflage has a place in Cather's writing, and at times she was writing two stories at once, a heterosexual and a homosexual one, just as she projected herself into both male and female characters. But the heterosexual story is not invariably the false one, the hidden lesbian story the real. And it would be reductive to envision all of Cather's writing as concealing lesbian subtexts, as well as minimizing her creative imagination. When there do seem to be two stories, I think it is fair to say that meaning and authorial intention can waver between the two. And the fact that Cather was a lesbian does not mean that all her characters are disguised lesbians. Like all great writers, she possessed a creative imagination that allowed her to create a variety of characters different from herself—people of different ethnicities, ages, occupations, genders, sexualities.

So while we need, as readers, to think about the connection between Willa Cather's life and her art, we need to remember that this connection is never simple or direct. There is no one-to-one correspondence to be found, even in novels that seem very autobiographical, such as *My Ántonia* or *The Song of the Lark*. Cather drew on her emotions and experience for her writing, but she also transformed these sources through her imagination.

When she first began writing fiction, however, Willa Cather did not yet possess the novelist's transforming power. Her apprenticeship fiction, which she began publishing during her college years, in general cannot be distinguished from the average fiction of her day. Many of her early stories are based on popular formulas or are more derived from her reading other writers than from her own observations. Occasionally, however, we can see signs of the later Willa Cather, as in her first published story, "Peter," which appeared in her college literary magazine in 1892. The story was based on the first tragic tale Cather had

WILLA CATHER

heard when she came to Nebraska: disheartened by a long, cold winter, Anton Sadilek, a Bohemian immigrant farmer, killed himself. He was the father of Annie Sadilek, the girl who would later be Cather's friend and the model for Ántonia. Although the short vignette "Peter," which Cather later reworked as the death of Mr. Shimerda in *My Ántonia,* gives a much darker view of Nebraska's harshness and immigrant despair than her novels would, it does anticipate her later fiction in its use of Nebraska memories.

Cather (center, touching tree) poses with several family members and childhood friends shortly before leaving Nebraska for Pittsburgh in 1896.

"THE THING NOT NAMED"

But as Cather moved eastward, she increasingly felt that Nebraska was not a "literary" enough setting for fiction. She began to place her characters in elegant Boston drawing rooms rather than behind the plow. It would take her 20 years before she returned to the subject matter she had received from her own past in *O Pioneers!,* the novel in which she fully and firmly created her voice as a writer.

Cather began her eastern pilgrimage shortly after her graduation from the University of Nebraska, reversing the pattern of her parents' migration as she moved first to Pittsburgh, then to New York City. After her graduation in 1895, she lived in Lincoln for several months, writing for the local newspapers. Then she moved home to Red Cloud and commuted back and forth to Lincoln throughout the spring of 1896. She felt restless and depressed during this year, particularly after her return home, which seemed confining and provincial after her free years in Lincoln. She suffered under the weight of other people's expectations: her friends and family seemed to be waiting for her to do something extraordinary, and she did not have much faith in her own resources.

Then a challenge came her way: she was offered the editorship of the *Home Monthly,* a new Pittsburgh-based women's magazine. Although it may seem paradoxical that the former William Cather would be heading a magazine intended for hearth, home, and the female reader, Willa Cather seized her chance. She left for Pittsburgh in the summer of 1896, eager to succeed as a professional journalist and ready to explore the world beyond Nebraska.

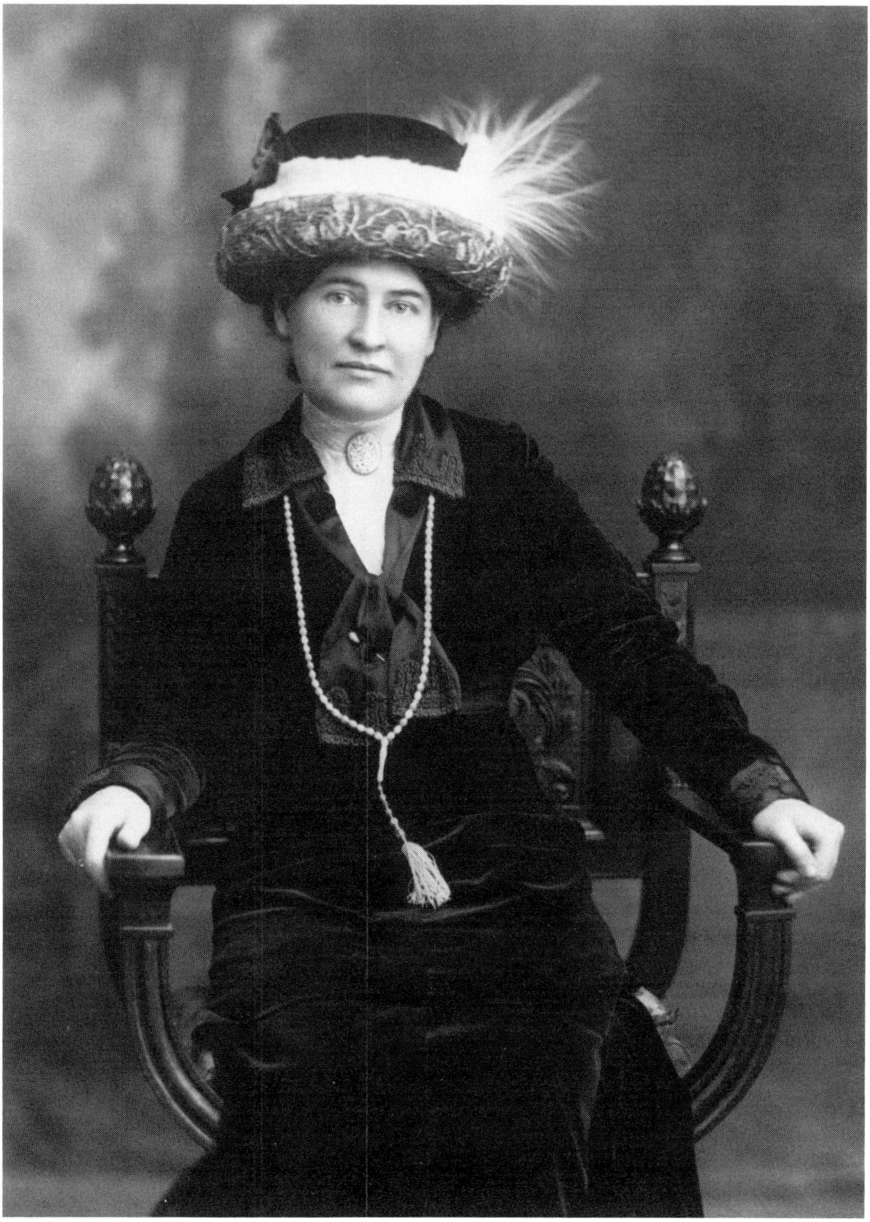

CHAPTER FOUR

THE EMERGING VOICE

Cather sports a necklace given to her by her literary mentor, the writer Sarah Orne Jewett. "Find a way of your own," Jewett advised her protégée. "If that way happens to be new, don't let that frighten you."

When Willa Cather moved to Pittsburgh in 1896 and took up the editorship of the *Home Monthly,* she began a successful career as a professional woman that brought her satisfaction, financial independence, and public recognition over the next several years. Ambitious and talented, she wanted to succeed in the masculine world outside the home, and succeed she eventually did—although at some personal cost. At first, the young Cather was insecure and uncertain; then, as years passed, she relaxed into a sense of her own competence and enjoyed her journalistic power and prestige. Finally, however, she felt exhausted and drained by her professional responsibilities and depressed that her own writing was not developing as she had hoped. Although she would publish several stories, a book of poems, and a short story collection between 1896 and 1912, she knew she had not found her own voice as a writer. In fact, when Cather was honored by an entry in *Who's Who* in 1909, she subtracted two years from her age, making her birth date 1875 instead of 1873. She felt that her literary promise had not kept pace with her age: perhaps if she were two years younger, she could expect less of herself as a writer.

Cather scoffed at the *Home Monthly*'s domestic content in a letter to Mariel Gere: it was the worst trash in the world, she told Mariel, all babies and mince pies. The articles and columns Cather selected for the first issue included household hints ("Table Points"), advice to young mothers ("Care of Children's First Teeth"), and moral uplift ("Christian Endeavor"). The magazine had pledged "pure and clean" entertainment for its female audience: no "unwholesome" fiction would be found in its pages.

Although Cather found the magazine's domestic slant unpalatable, she was determined to succeed at her job. If it was trash they wanted, it was trash they would have, she wrote to Gere—the very best trash she could produce. She wrote some stories herself for the magazine, and although they are far from trash, Cather was forced to conform, at least on the surface, to the popular fictional formulas of the day. As her friend Edith Lewis reflected, Cather did not explore her own original gifts during her time at the *Home Monthly,* having to produce conventional stories "which had little relation to her own thinking and feeling."

While Lewis's point is largely true, in one story—"Tommy, the Unsentimental"—Cather managed to challenge the expectations of popular ladies' fiction by writing a narrative in which a tomboy heroine, much like the younger Willa, triumphs over the clinging, dependent Miss Jessica, a stereotype of the delicate female virtues praised elsewhere in the magazine. But for the most part, Cather wrote in popular genres, with one eye on her publisher and employer and another on the middle-class female readers whom she was supposed to please. She did well as an editor but did not find the *Home Monthly* a space for developing a personal voice.

The magazine changed ownership while Cather was in Red Cloud in the summer of 1897, and she resigned. She then secured a newspaper job, editing wire copy on the telegraph desk of the Pittsburgh *Leader.*

THE EMERGING VOICE

Back in the city, she also continued to write book and drama reviews for the *Home Monthly,* the *Leader,* and Lincoln newspapers.

Cather continued at the *Leader* until early 1900, when she left to freelance for the *Library,* a new and short-lived literary journal. In March 1901, she took a job teaching Latin at Pittsburgh's Central High School; and in the fall of 1901, Cather moved into the English department, where she remained for two years before transferring to Allegheny High School. She taught English at Allegheny until she left Pittsburgh in 1906 for New York and the final stage of her journalistic career, working for *McClure's Magazine.*

The articles and reviews Willa Cather wrote during her Pittsburgh years—some for the *Home Monthly* and the Pittsburgh *Leader,* others for Lincoln newspapers—show that although she had abandoned her William Cather persona, she continued to show contempt for "ordinary" women who conformed to the 19th-century ideology of femininity. She ridiculed the women's literary clubs and reading circles that were springing up in the 1890s, charging that women had "no particular talent for good fellowship," and found the female idea that literary culture could be nibbled along with cucumber sandwiches, or sipped along with afternoon tea, "just a little ludicrous." Still identifying with masculine values, Cather thought that women inevitably trivialized high culture.

Her favorite target was the *Ladies' Home Journal,* which she attacked in an 1896 column. This "organ of exquisite literary culture," Cather wrote with heavy irony, would juxtapose breathless praise of Shakespeare or Dante with hints about the latest fashions, or unashamedly follow an article on Ludwig van Beethoven with advice to readers on whether "it is proper to kiss a young man good night after returning from a party." Such debasement of literary and artistic subjects was a feminine trait, Cather charged.

Throughout her Pittsburgh years, Cather also continued to believe that woman and artist were contradictory identities, a conviction that was another barrier to her own literary emergence. She admired women opera singers and actresses, but she felt that most women writers had not risen above feminine mediocrity. Such writers limited themselves

WILLA CATHER

Surrounded by books and papers, Cather works in an office in Pittsburgh. At this point in her career, she was quite successful as an editor at the *Home Monthly* and published a number of her own stories in the magazine. Yet she despised the magazine's prudish morality and oppressive attitude toward women.

to romantic and domestic plots, making Cather impatient with their inability to transcend typical, and limiting, female roles. "As a rule," she wrote in an 1897 review, "if I see the announcement of a new book by a woman, I—well, I take one by a man instead. . . . I have noticed that the great masters of letters are men, and I prefer to take no chances when I read."

Cather did acknowledge some exceptional women writers, however; she admired "the great Georges, George Eliot and George Sand, and they were anything but women, and there was Miss [Charlotte] Bronte who kept her sentimentality under control, and there was Jane Austen who certainly had more common sense than any of them and was in some respects the greatest of them all." Even here, however, Cather suggests that femininity and literary greatness are incompatible, characterizing the "great Georges" as "anything but women." And her literary advice to young women writers further suggests that she connected literary excellence with masculinity: "Women are so horribly subjective and they have such a scorn for the healthy commonplace. When a woman writes a story of adventure, a stout sea tale, a manly battle yarn, anything without wine, women and love, then I will begin to hope for something great from them, not before."

Cather's advice did not contain useful literary wisdom, given that writers generally do best when they draw upon what they know or want to imagine. Not many women would have had experience of stout sea voyages or manly battles, and when Cather attempted a battle yarn herself, in her World War I novel *One of Ours* (1922), she created perhaps her most unconvincing novel.

So even as Willa Cather had given up her William Cather persona, during her Pittsburgh years her male impersonation continued in a more subtle fashion, as masculine values continued to shape her artistic values and beliefs.

Nevertheless, Cather's Pittsburgh period was an important time of transition in her views of gender. Although her praise of masculine aesthetic values and male writers persisted, at the same time she was developing an important friendship with a woman who would help her to understand the value of female intimacy, to enjoy feminine dress, and ultimately to appreciate the womanhood she would shape for herself. Isabelle McClung was the beautiful, aristocratic daughter of a Pittsburgh judge, and she would be the romantic love of Cather's life.

When Cather first arrived in Pittsburgh, she lived in a series of boardinghouses, feeling lonely and uprooted. But in 1899, her life changed when she met Isabelle McClung. Isabelle was a lover of the arts, and she and Cather met because of their common friendship with an actress. The two women quickly became close friends, and Cather was a frequent guest at the McClung mansion on Murray Hill Avenue. In 1901, Isabelle ended her friend's transient boardinghouse life when she asked Cather to live with her. Cather would stay with Isabelle, sharing a bedroom, until she left for New York in 1906.

The McClungs' reactions to their daughter's invitation and their permanent houseguest differ, depending on who is telling the story. According to Cather's first biographer, E. K. Brown, the parents did not welcome the new guest, but their daughter reportedly threatened to leave home and they gave in. A McClung grandson remembers that Cather's presence caused a strain in the household. But Willa Cather's sister Elsie and her niece Helen Cather Southwick portray the household arrangement as harmonious for everyone.

It is difficult to sort out these conflicting stories or to determine why the McClungs might initially have opposed Cather's entrance into their household. They need not have interpreted their daughter's relationship as lesbian to have been disturbed by it; Isabelle was at a marriageable age, and the parents must have realized that her new intimacy signified a lack of interest in men. The McClungs may simply not have wanted their lives and family patterns disrupted by a stranger, particularly one as independent and opinionated as Cather. But eventually she became an adopted member of the family.

Even while living within a family, Cather and Isabelle McClung found time for privacy and intimacy. As a Pittsburgh friend recalls in her memoir: "The two young women would forsake the family group soon after dinner, and evening after evening would go upstairs to the bedroom they shared to read together in quiet. This room was at the back of the house and its wide low window gave on a downward slope across gardens and shaded streets toward the Monongahela river and the green hills rising beyond. There were no close neighbours to destroy their sense of privacy. Here the friends . . . devoured the novels of Tolstoi, Turgenev, Balzac, and Flaubert."

While the bedroom the two women shared reflects their intimacy, another room Cather enjoyed shows how Isabelle supported her friend's creativity. On the third floor, there was an unused sewing room that Cather took over as a study and writing room. Like the attic bedroom

THE EMERGING VOICE

she enjoyed in Red Cloud, this space allowed Cather the solitude she needed to pursue her imaginative life. Yet it was solitude without loneliness, for once she was through with writing for the evening, she could return to her companionship with Isabelle.

Just as Isabelle fostered her friend's writing, so she helped her to reconcile creativity with femininity. Isabelle was a beautiful, elegant woman who enjoyed fine clothes and enjoyed buying them for Cather. Under Isabelle's tutelage, Cather became more interested in elegant styles of women's dress. In later years, Cather would purchase "lovely fabrics, furs, and beautiful hats" from Bergdorf Goodman's and have dresses custom-made. She tended to prefer royal and theatrical clothing—velvets and silks, turbans and feathers, which became signs of female power to her.

Cather wrote several stories and poems while she lived with Isabelle and published a book of poems in 1903 (*April Twilights*). In the same year, her fiction caught the eye of S. S. McClure, the powerful editor of *McClure's Magazine*. He published two of Cather's stories in his magazine ("Paul's Case" and "The Sculptor's Funeral"), and in 1905 his publishing company brought out Cather's first collection of stories, *The Troll Garden*. Cather was in awe of McClure: she felt grateful for his attention and praise. Perhaps he would be the mentor who would help her achieve the literary career she wanted.

But McClure had another destiny in mind for Cather. He thought she would make a good reporter and editor, and he wanted her to work for him. In 1906, he offered her a job as a staff writer for *McClure's*. Although it must have been painful for Cather to leave Pittsburgh, she could not turn down this offer. She knew she could return for visits with Isabelle, and Isabelle could visit her in New York. So, in the summer of 1906, Cather left Pittsburgh for New York City to begin working with McClure, who turned out to be a professional rather than a literary mentor.

S. S. McClure was a self-made man, a dynamic editor who in addition to founding the important muckraking and literary journal *McClure's* had fostered the careers of such well-known writers as Lincoln Steffens and Ida Tarbell. McClure was a brilliant editor but a hard man to work for; his chaotic energy and relentless cascade of ideas could make it difficult for his writers to focus on their stories. In 1906, his best staff writers, including Steffens and Tarbell, quit to form a rival publication, and McClure had to rebuild his organization, so he convinced Cather to return to journalism. Within a short time, she moved from staff writer to managing editor, becoming a powerful force at one of the nation's best-known and most respected periodicals as well as a recognized figure in the New York, Boston, and London literary worlds. Success at *McClure's* meant success according to the rules American society laid out for men, and Cather still wanted success on those terms.

On the surface, Cather's years at *McClure's* were years of heady accomplishment. Her position brought her many advantages: she was able to publish several of her own stories in the magazine; she traveled to England to develop contacts with writers, including such literary greats as Ford Madox Ford and H. G. Wells; she bought fiction from such established American writers as Jack London and Theodore Dreiser and encouraged unknowns such as Zoë Akins, who eventually became one of her closest friends. Those times when Cather pulled off a publishing coup, as when she captured actress Ellen Terry's memoirs for *McClure's,* she "felt the job was worth all it cost her." Her working relationship with S. S. McClure was close and supportive: he thought she was a brilliant journalist and trusted her completely; she, in turn, gave him her admiration, loyalty, and respect.

And yet these powerful years at *McClure's,* when Cather was riding the crest of her professional wave, were also years of sudden illnesses. In her letters to McClure, she frequently apologized for being waylaid by infections or flus. These illnesses were signs of emotional distress that increased along with Cather's editorial success. Although she struck others as energetic, confident, and self-assured, she progressively felt depleted, exhausted, and unsure of her literary talents. Her job was demanding and left her drained at the end of the day, unable to face her own writing. And because her work involved securing and editing other people's manuscripts, she was paradoxically enabling other people to write while she was silencing herself.

THE EMERGING VOICE

Cather's relationship with McClure also contributed to her dilemma. Although she might have struck some observers as powerfully masculine in her decisiveness and assurance, in fact she was playing the very feminine role of the good daughter in relation to her professional father. McClure admired and praised her as a journalist, which was the vocation that he found useful. He ceased to flatter Cather as a fiction writer and eventually downplayed her fiction, suggesting to her that her true talents were in editing—doubtless because he wanted her to continue working for him.

Cather, in turn, wanted to please McClure, but to do so she had to stay within the role that was draining her creative energy and undermining her artistic self-confidence. She could not see how his self-interest was being served by flattering her as a journalist and undermining her as a writer. He was her mirror, and she trusted the reflection she saw.

In 1908, Cather wrote a discouraged and depressed letter to Sarah Orne Jewett, the Maine author who was to be the maternal mentor of Cather's fiction writing. Cather honestly confessed her self-doubts to the older woman. With all her energy absorbed by work she did not want to be doing, after a day in the office she simply did not have the resources to write, she told Jewett. Cather felt like a broken circuit. She was not yet 34 years old and should be a better fiction writer than she was, she confided, but when she tried to write a story, she felt like a newborn baby every time. (Small wonder, then, that Cather decided to turn the clock back for her 1909 *Who's Who* entry, subtracting two years from her age, as if that way she could give herself more time to develop as a writer.)

Cather was not without literary accomplishments, however. By 1911, when she took a leave of absence from *McClure's* to write, in addition to *April Twilights* and *The Troll Garden* she had published dozens of stories in respected periodicals such as the *Century, Harper's,* and the *Atlantic* as well as *McClure's*. Some of her fiction, generally that which drew most deeply on her observation and memory, combined literary craft with emotional power, and stories such as "Paul's Case," "The Sculptor's Funeral," "A Wagner Matinée," and "The Sentimentality of William Tavener" are among her best.

WILLA CATHER

During these same years, Cather was not fully writing in her own voice. She had fallen under the spell of Henry James, known then as the master of American fiction. The expatriated James, who lived in England and chose international settings for his fiction, had little in common with the Nebraska-born Cather. Yet she strove to imitate his elegant, cerebral, controlled fiction, filling her stories with upper-middle-class characters, country estates, and stilted dialogue.

Remembering those times, Cather later observed that the "drawing-room was considered the proper setting for a novel, and the only characters worth reading about were smart people or clever people." Imitating James in stories such as "The Willing Muse" and "Eleanor's House," she was conforming to elite literary conventions preferred by the eastern establishment of publishers, critics, and reviewers. Speaking in James's rhythms, using his elevated and abstract vocabulary, borrowing his settings, Cather was not creating what she later attributed to Sarah Orne Jewett, a fresh and vital language, a "quality of voice that is exclusively the writer's own, individual, unique." As Cather later said in speaking of her Jamesian period, "I was trying to sing a song that did not lie in my voice."

In part, Cather was being subservient to Henry James because he was America's most admired living novelist, and in part because she wanted to distance herself as much as possible from women writers whom she did not respect. She was still not sure that woman and writer could be compatible identities.

Both a woman and a writer herself, Sarah Orne Jewett helped Willa Cather to see that these identities could coexist. Jewett was a guide for Cather at the crucial transitional moment in her life, supporting her as she was finding her true vocation as a writer and her literary "road home" to Nebraska. A very different mirror from McClure, Jewett reflected to Cather the image of herself as a gifted fiction writer.

Cather met Jewett in 1908 at the gracious Boston home of Annie Fields. The widow of Boston publisher James Fields, Mrs. Fields was a literary figure in her own right: writer, memoirist, and literary hostess, she had done much to encourage women writers. She and Jewett became good friends and then lifelong partners after James Fields

THE EMERGING VOICE

The friendship and guidance of Sarah Orne Jewett was invaluable to Cather's development as a writer. A confident, established lesbian writer, Jewett was an important role model for Cather, being a significant corrective to the accepted notion of women as heterosexual and noncreative.

died, forming one of the Boston marriages common in 19th-century America.

When Cather met Jewett, the older woman looked familiar, and Cather realized she had seen her before: Jewett "looked very like the youthful picture of herself in the game of 'Authors' I had played as a child," Cather recalled, "except that she was fuller in figure and a little grey." This remembered detail reveals why Jewett was so important to Cather. She was a recognized "author," like the famous male writers who dominated the Authors cards: Nathaniel Hawthorne, Henry Wadsworth Longfellow, John Greenleaf Whittier. And yet Jewett was a woman, one who, unlike Cather, had never tried to be "anything but" a woman. In fact, as Cather later observed, Jewett was a "lady, in the old high sense"—a cultured, self-assured woman born to a heritage of breeding, refinement, and reliable income.

WILLA CATHER

Cather had admired Jewett's work when she first encountered it in the 1890s. By 1908, Jewett was a respected American writer whose *The Country of the Pointed Firs* (1897), a series of interlocking sketches about a small Maine community, was widely considered the high-water mark of local-color fiction, a genre of late 19th-century writing in which the particularities of place, culture, and community were featured. Jewett's fiction was admired by writers such as Rudyard Kipling, William Dean Howells, and Cather's literary father, Henry James. Jewett was, Cather told her friend Elizabeth Sergeant, America's "best woman writer."

Although Jewett was 25 years older than Cather and outranked the younger woman in age, literary achievements, and social class, their brief friendship, which lasted until Jewett's death in 1909, was marked by mutuality and reciprocity. Jewett was the catalyst to Cather's emerging creativity, while Cather gave the older woman the chance to be a mentor and to find a literary inheritor. Unlike Cather's bond with her own mother, this was a mother-daughter relationship that was not marred by inequality or hierarchy: the friendship flowed both ways.

Cather shared some of her fiction with Jewett, and Jewett in return offered support and gentle criticism. Cather had shown her "On the Gull's Road," an early Jamesian story in which Cather uses a male narrator to explore the mesmerizing power of a maternal woman, as she would later do, with far more success, in *My Ántonia*. Jewett, who had written many stories about women, almost always used female narrators. Because she had come of age during the era when romantic women's friendships were more socially accepted, she never felt she had to camouflage a story of love or romantic attachment by casting one of the characters as male. So she thought Cather had made a mistake in using a male narrator. Notice, however, how delicately Jewett suggests an alternative, and how much appreciation she shows for Cather's literary gifts:

> And now I wish to tell you . . . with what deep happiness and recognition I have read the "McClure" story,—night before last I found it with surprise and delight. . . . It makes me the more sure that you are far on your road

THE EMERGING VOICE

to a fine and long story of very high class. The lover is as well done as he could be when a woman writes in the man's character,—it must always, I believe, be something of a masquerade. . . . And you could almost have done it as yourself—a woman could love her in that same protecting way—a woman could even care enough to take her away from such a life, by some means or other. But oh, how close—how tender—how true the feeling is! The sea air blows through the very letters on the page. Do not hurry too fast in these early winter days,—a quiet hour is worth more to you than anything you can do in it.

Cather was not able to follow Jewett's advice immediately. It still seemed preferable to Cather—in the changed social climate in which the word *unnatural* was used to condemn women's romantic friendships—to view powerful women through male eyes, as she did in *My Ántonia* and again in *A Lost Lady*. But when she was more self-assured, Cather did take up the challenge of presenting a charismatic older woman through the eyes of a younger woman—in *My Mortal Enemy*—and perhaps she thought of Jewett when she did so.

In December 1908, Jewett sent Cather the most important letter she ever received. "I think it became a permanent inhabitant of her thoughts," Edith Lewis observed. It is a wonderful letter—a letter of both encouragement and warning. Jewett was concerned that Cather's demanding work at the magazine was impeding her literary development, and she had the delicate task of letting the younger woman know she was concerned about her literary growth without disheartening her. Sensitive to the emotional response of her reader, Jewett managed the task well:

My dear Willa,—

I have been thinking about you and hoping that things are going well. I cannot help saying what I think about your writing and its being hindered by such incessant, important, responsible work as you have in your hands now. I do think it is impossible for you to work so hard and yet have your gifts mature as they should. . . . I do wish in my heart that the force of this year could have gone into three or four stories. In the "Troll-Garden" the Sculptor's Funeral stands alone a head higher than the rest, and it is to that level you must hold and take for a starting-point. You are older now than that book in general; you have been living and reading and knowing new types; but if you don't keep and guard and mature your force, and above all, have time and quiet to perfect your work, you will be writing things not much better than you did five years ago. This you are anxiously saying to yourself! but I am wondering how to get at the right conditions.

Jewett knew that Cather's magazine work was taking time and "force" away from her writing, and she also felt that Cather did not possess sufficient control over her material. What Cather needed to do to improve her writing, Jewett thought, was paradoxical. She needed both to be "surer" of her "backgrounds" and to see her material more "from the outside." This advice struck home, as Cather explained in 1922: "One of the few really helpful words I ever heard from an older writer, I had from Sarah Orne Jewett when she said to me: 'Of course, one day you will write about your own country. In the meantime, get all you can. One must know the world *so well* before one can know the parish.'"

After Cather had looked back to Nebraska and learned, after seeing the world, to know the parish, she always connected her literary self-discovery to Jewett's advice and influence. Shortly after *O Pioneers!* appeared, Cather attributed her return to Nebraska material to Jewett, "who had read all my early stories and had very clear and definite opinions about where my work fell short. She said, 'Write it as it is, don't try to make it like this or that. You can't do it in anybody else's way—you will have to find a way of your own. If that way happens to be new, don't let that frighten you. Don't try to write the kind of short story that this or that magazine wants—write the truth, and let them take it or leave it.'"

As she urged Cather toward self-expression, Jewett wanted her to find a protective, nurturing solitude: "To work in silence and with all one's heart, that is the writer's lot; he is the only artist who must be a solitary, and yet needs the widest outlook in the world." And yet the artist only need be a "solitary" in the act of writing; the rest of life could, and should, be filled with supportive friendships. So Jewett also encouraged Cather to find a "quiet place near the best companions (not those who admire and wonder at everything one does, but those who know the good things with delight!)."

Jewett ended her letter by reassuring the younger woman that she had been "growing" even when she felt "most hindered," and reminding Cather that she was not alone: "I have been full of thought about you." Later, Cather would acknowledge Jewett's maternal role in her literary emergence when she dedicated *O Pioneers!* to her. It was a fitting gesture, for in this novel Cather united the world and the parish.

In her support and in her advice, Jewett let Cather know that creativity and companionship could coexist; the writer needed both solitude and intimacy, and in fact writing with friends in mind, as one writes a letter, could help the writer to work. After Cather hit her stride as a novelist, she said that her friend Isabelle McClung was the one person for whom all her books had been written, the ideal reader who kept her company in the loneliness of the creative act. Jewett's view that creativity and relationship not only could coexist but could support each other countered the romantic, and the American, image of the lonely, isolated artist—an image that Cather had once held, an image that may be more compatible with male-defined aesthetics than with women's creative and emotional needs. "If an artist does any good work he must do it alone," she wrote during her college years. "No number of encouraging or admiring friends can assist him, they retard him rather." Certainly, this model of the lonely artist did not fit with Cather's artistic and personal temperament. Friendship and intimacy gave her the emotional atmosphere she needed in order to write. During periods when she felt lonely, isolated, or uprooted, her creative work suffered.

Fortunately for Cather, she did not need to choose between writing and companionship: she found several friends and lovers who, in different and complementary ways, nourished her creativity. Recognizing the "good things with delight," these women provided emotional and professional support during Cather's apprenticeship years as well as during the crucial transitional time when she was moving from the role of professional woman to that of writer.

WILLA CATHER

Most important to Cather's life and writing during these early years was Isabelle McClung. Isabelle was more interested in fostering her friend's creativity than in developing her own, so Cather felt no competition in this relationship. The dedication Cather included with *The Song of the Lark* (1915), her portrait of the artist as a young woman, conveys Isabelle's role in her creative life through the metaphor of the garden, with all its connotations of cultivation, care, and joyous growth:

> TO
> ISABELLE McCLUNG
> On uplands,
> At morning,
> The world was young, the winds were free;
> A garden fair,
> In that blue desert air,
> Its guest invited me to be.

Isabelle remained the "garden fair" for Willa Cather even after she moved to New York. The two women maintained their close relationship, frequently vacationing together, and Cather would travel to Pittsburgh for long visits, writing portions of *O Pioneers!* and *The Song of the Lark* there. Isabelle also came to New York. A mutual friend remembers her in Willa's Bank Street apartment, where she "cast a glow which was reflected in Willa's shining face."

But in New York, Edith Lewis gradually became more and more important to Cather. Cather once explained that she needed to work "in a corner protected by someone who knew what it was all about," and she mentioned both Isabelle McClung and Edith Lewis as her protectors. Lewis could not offer Cather a gracious Pittsburgh mansion, but she knew how to create the emotional and psychological sanctuary Cather needed to write.

Cather had met Lewis, who was working for a New York publisher, on a visit to Lincoln in 1903. They struck up a friendship, which Cather renewed when she first came to New York. In 1908, the two women set up their own apartment at 82 Washington Place, and in 1913 they began housekeeping at 5 Bank Street, the Greenwich Village apartment

THE EMERGING VOICE

where Cather spent some of her happiest, most productive years. They were to be lifelong partners, spending almost 40 years together.

At Bank Street, Lewis and Cather created another "garden fair." A spacious, sunny, apartment, Bank Street was a harmonious, almost sacred space to Cather. Entering her apartment was like walking into a greenhouse—the air was sensuous, at any season filled with the perfume of fresh cut flowers: orange blossoms and camellias in the winter, jonquils and lilacs in the spring. Here Cather and Lewis also loved to entertain, giving "at homes" on Friday afternoon to their circle of artistic and literary friends.

Bank Street was the "walled stronghold of her very self," as Elizabeth Sergeant observed, and when Cather was forced to relocate in 1927 she felt "exposed and miserable," like a turtle without its shell. Cather did not create this sheltering home alone: Lewis was her essential companion. Their tastes were similar. After they had decorated the apartment

Isabelle McClung (left), Cather, and their guide, camping out in Wyoming in 1905.
Cather revered McClung's intelligence, beauty, and social grace, while McClung did her utmost to foster Cather's writing.

with mahogany chests and a dining room table, they agreed to give "no more thought to acquiring new things," Lewis recalled in her memoir, *Willa Cather Living*. "The money we had we preferred to spend on flowers, music, and entertaining our friends." They also agreed that the services of a French housekeeper were essential; Cather had a refined taste in food and wine, and she found Josephine Bourda, who worked at Bank Street for several years and cooked lunches for Cather, an intangible asset to her creativity.

Most observers of the couple saw Cather as the dominant partner. One friend described Cather as the captain, Lewis as the first mate. Certainly, it was clear to both women that Cather's career and needs took precedence. Lewis worked in publishing and advertising, managing her own career very well; but she also played the part of the traditional literary wife, helping Cather by correcting proofs, fending off unwanted visitors, making travel arrangements, and generally serving as a buffer between Cather and the outside world. In addition to removing these burdens, Lewis refrained from making excessive demands on her friend's time. She was available when needed, absent when not, as when she would accompany Cather on western vacations but return to New York when Cather was ready to stop off in Red Cloud to see her parents and childhood friends.

It is easy to assume that Lewis played a less important role in Cather's life than did Isabelle McClung. It is true that Isabelle was her grand romance, her muse, her ideal reader, in part because the two women never had to confront the sometimes unromantic reality of a shared life; Cather's separation from Isabelle kept her feelings quite intense. Cather imagined herself writing all her books for Isabelle and dedicated *The Song of the Lark* to her, and yet she did not dedicate any books to the woman with whom she was living and who was dutifully checking proofs with her.

Cather, however, wanted to be buried beside Edith Lewis. During the 1940s, Cather made it clear to family members that she was not going to be buried in Red Cloud but in Jaffrey, New Hampshire, the summer retreat associated both with her writing and with Lewis, who accompanied her to the Shattuck Inn for many summers. Those who

THE EMERGING VOICE

Edith Lewis poses for a Smith College yearbook photo in 1902. An intelligent, dedicated friend who strongly supported Cather's writing, Lewis provided Cather with both companionship and editing expertise for almost 40 years.

seek the grave site may find further evidence of Lewis's subordination to Cather: her gravestone is smaller and humbler. Yet the juxtaposition of the graves also tells the story of Lewis's importance to Cather, along with the story of a relationship in which each woman maintained a separate identity. The story of the graves suggests that Lewis's place in Cather's emotional and creative life was not subordinate to Isabelle's but different, and quite likely equally important. She gave Cather a sustaining relationship and living environment in which to do her creative work, and that is not an insignificant gift.

WILLA CATHER

Many other women friends supported Cather at different times during her literary career. Elizabeth Sergeant, a young writer and journalist, knew Cather during the *McClure's* years. The two women became acquainted when Sergeant submitted an article to Cather, and they quickly moved beyond the editor-writer relationship to a close friendship. Sergeant, who admired Cather's writing and encouraged her shift from journalism to full-time fiction writing, was particularly important as a reader of *O Pioneers!* Cather was insecure about the new direction her fiction was taking, and Sergeant assured her that this

Cather crosses a creek in Virginia. Although she lived most of her life in the urban environment of New York City, she returned frequently to the more rural locales of her childhood and was an experienced outdoorswoman.

THE EMERGING VOICE

Nebraska novel had power and originality. When Cather gave her a copy of the published book, she inscribed it "To Elsie Sergeant, the first friend of this book."

Other "best companions," as Jewett had hoped, nurtured Cather's life and writing: playwright Zoë Akins; opera singer Olive Fremstad; novelists Sigrid Undset and Zona Gale; and, particularly important in the 1920s, Cather's regained college friend and fellow writer Dorothy Canfield Fisher. Thus, while Cather wrote alone and in solitude, she was sustained and supported by women friends who played many roles: protectors, catalysts, muses, critics, supporters.

Cather had excellent working relationships with her male editors and publishers, Ferris Greenslet of Houghton Mifflin and later Alfred Knopf, and she made good use of Paul Reynolds, her literary agent. But her sympathetic female supporters were more important to her creativity. The literary men in her life tended to come into play after Cather had completed a novel, while the women were entwined with the creative process.

The support of Sarah Orne Jewett, Isabelle McClung, Edith Lewis, and Elizabeth Sergeant was particularly crucial during the difficult transitional period 1908–12, when Cather was building up her confidence and courage in order to disappoint S. S. McClure, leave the magazine, and take the risk of committing herself to writing, all the time fearful that she might not succeed at what she most wanted to do: write a novel.

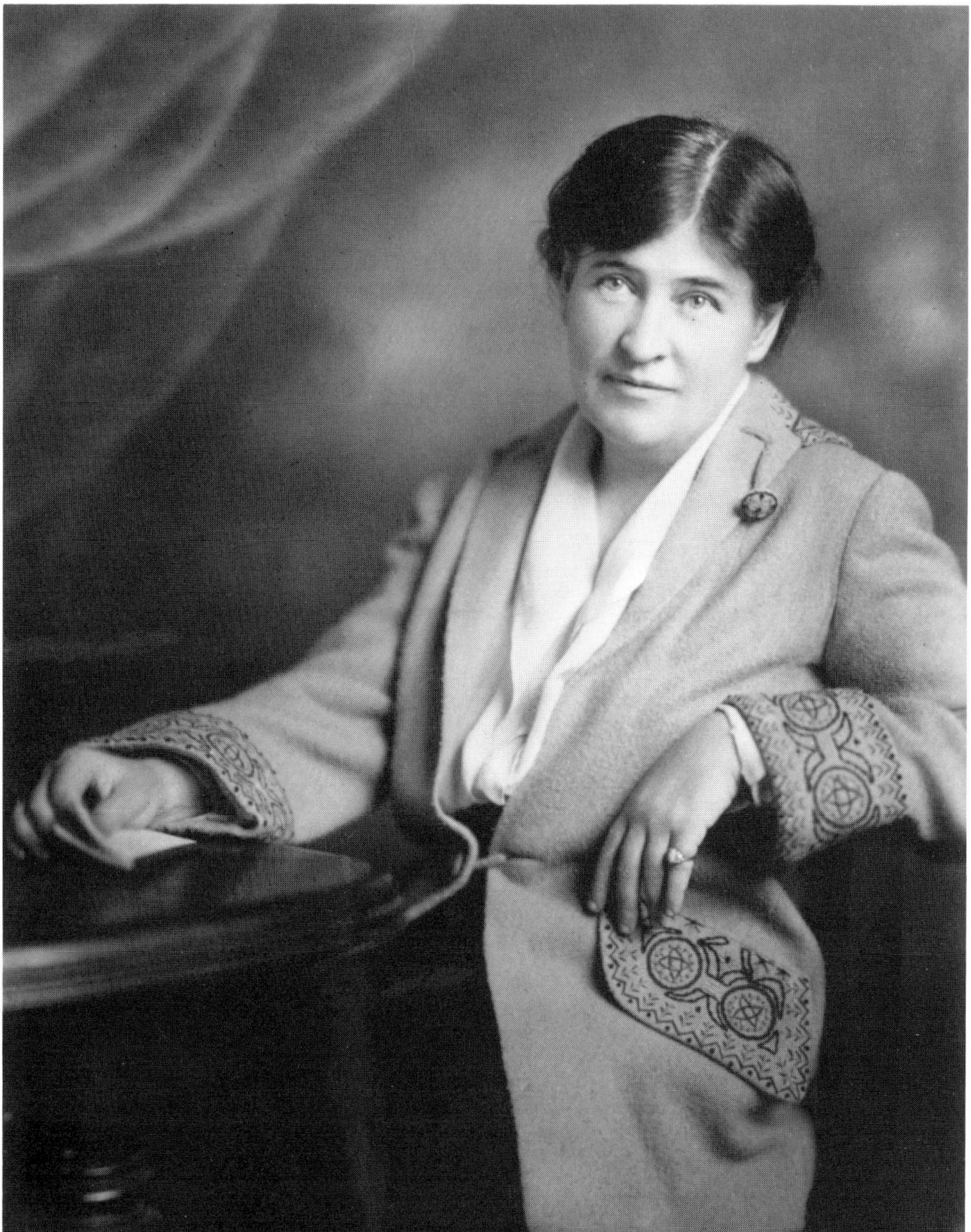

CHAPTER FIVE

EVERY ARTIST MAKES HERSELF BORN

In the fall of 1911, Willa Cather took a short leave from her work at *McClure's Magazine*. She and Isabelle McClung went to Cherry Valley, New York, a small village in the Finger Lakes region. The two women rented a house, and Cather spent her time sleeping, eating, hiking, and writing, recovering from the stress of her demanding job. She had been working on a novel, *Alexander's Bridge,* and managed to finish it during this time. But the novel was still in her Henry Jamesian mode, an "external" story, as she said later, that did not spring from her deepest self. Set in Boston and London drawing rooms, the novel shows Cather's continuing desire to follow dominant literary fashions.

During this vacation, Cather also wrote two stories that pointed in new directions—back toward her Nebraska roots and forward toward her literary future. She published "The Bohemian Girl," a love story set on the Nebraska Divide, in 1912; but "Alexandra," the story of a Scandinavian farm woman, did not seem complete, and she set it aside. She did not yet know it, but she was on her way to *O Pioneers!*

Cather relaxes at her desk. In the second decade of the 20th century, she developed from an insecure and imitative writer to a successful, well-respected artist with a unique perspective and voice.

Cather's restorative vacation at Cherry Valley, combined with the fact that Houghton Mifflin accepted *Alexander's Bridge* for publication, gave her the courage to take an even longer and more important break from *McClure's,* a break that would become permanent. In 1912, she decided to take a journey to the Southwest, and this journey was to be the turning point in her creative life.

Cather envisioned her trip to the Southwest as a vacation. She had been ill for several weeks in early 1912 and needed rejuvenation, so she decided to visit her brother Douglass, who was working on the Santa Fe railroad and stationed in Winslow, Arizona. When she set off from New York, for the first time in years she was not thinking about work or accomplishment. S. S. McClure approved of her trip; *Alexander's Bridge* was being published; she had done some good new writing at Cherry Valley. So as the train headed west, Cather could open herself up to the experiences awaiting her. Her work done, she was ready to play.

In Winslow, Willa and Douglass explored canyons and Indian cliff dwellings, saw an Indian ritual—the Hopi snake dance—and rode, hiked, and camped. It was wonderful being with Douglass, Cather wrote to McClure. They were having adventures together, just as they had in childhood.

While staying with her brother, Cather spent a good deal of time with a young Mexican named Julio who was living in Winslow's Spanish settlement. He sang Mexican love songs, took Cather to the Painted Desert, and escorted her to a Mexican dance, where she was the only Anglo woman. He also told her local legends and myths. Cather was infatuated with Julio, and her letters back to Elizabeth Sergeant are joyous, exuberant, glowing. These letters do not tell us whether she and Julio actually became lovers, or even how much attention and time he really gave her. What they do tell us is that Cather experienced love's intense emotional range: rapture, wonder, self-abandonment, self-renewal.

Cather was also captured by the Southwest's desert landscape and by the Indian cultures she found there. In some ways, the Southwest's terrain, which mingles the vast open spaces of desert and sky with the enclosed spaces of canyons and mesas, combined the best of Nebraska and Virginia, the two landscapes of Cather's past. The new landscape was similar to Nebraska in its immensity of scale, but its mesas, plateaus, and mountains intervened between the self and the horizon, as had Virginia's Blue Ridge Mountains, forming the boundaries and barriers Nebraska lacked. Cather's portrayals of the Southwest in *The Song of the Lark, The Professor's House,* and *Death Comes for the Archbishop* are filled with such paradoxical spaces, suggesting the connection between this landscape and her creative process. In the Southwest, as in her writing, Cather could be at once adventurous and protected, risk taking and safe, open and boundaried.

Like other writers and artists who gravitated to the Southwest during the first decades of the 20th century—novelists D. H. Lawrence and Mary Austin, photographer Laura Gilpin, writer and literary figure Mabel Dodge Luhan—Cather was enthralled by Pueblo civilization. Communal, ritualistic, mystic, the Southwest Indians' culture seemed a healthy counterpoint to the increasing individualism and materialism of American life. Writing later of southwestern culture, in particular of the ancient cliff dwellers' civilization, Cather was drawn to people who imbued daily life with order and meaning: "When you see those ancient pyramidical pueblos once more brought nearer by the sunset light that beats on them like gold-beaters' hammers, when the aromatic piñon smoke begins to curl up in the still air and the boys bring in the cattle and the old Indians come out in their white burnouses and take their accustomed grave positions upon the housetops, you begin to feel that custom, ritual, integrity of tradition have a reality that goes deeper than the bustling business of the world."

In the harmonious relationship the Indians enjoyed with their environment, Cather saw enacted the creative process to which she was moving. The Indians seemed "not to have struggled to overcome their environment," she noted approvingly, but adapted to its requirements: "They accommodated themselves to it, interpreted it and made it personal; lived in a dignified relation with it. In more senses than one they built themselves into it. . . . House building, in those great natural arches of stone, was but carrying out a suggestion that stared them in the face. . . . When they felled cedars with stone axes they were but accelerating a natural process."

In Cather's fiction, as in the writings of many other American authors, house building and houses are often metaphors for the creative process and for art. So the native artisans whose dwellings she saw in the Southwest built their houses the way Cather was beginning to fashion her stories: not by imposing their designs upon subject matter, but by accommodating to the forms and shapes that were already present; not by importing foreign materials (like the writer who imitated others' methods, as Cather had imitated Henry James), but by working with the material that had been given them. When Cather allowed the art to emerge from her Nebraska past, she, like the Indians, was carrying out a suggestion that had "stared [her] in the face" but that she had been unable to see—her eyes were so intent on professional achievement and

Bishop John Baptist Lamy, the first Roman Catholic bishop in the American Southwest, became the model for the hero of Cather's *Death Comes for the Archbishop*.

elite eastern and European literary culture, she was blind to the literary power of her own heritage.

Cather was particularly moved by the pots and vessels the Indians had shaped to hold grain and water. She felt initiated into a female artistic tradition, for the potters had been women who crafted their beautiful yet functional vessels from the earth. She felt inspired by "women who, under conditions of incredible difficulty and fear of enemies had still designed and molded . . . beautiful objects for daily use out of river-bottom clay." In the cliff dwellers' civilization, unlike her own, woman and artist were not conflicting identities. Following so soon after her literary inheritance from Sarah Orne Jewett, Cather's discovery of the Indian women potters strengthened her association of femaleness with creativity.

Simultaneously, Cather began to see that art could come from the earth, from the materials of daily life, from the soil of the Southwest or from the soil of Nebraska. And because the pot is an ancient female symbol—its open, receptive space echoing the female body, the womb, and the female genitals—Cather could concretely see the connections among women's generative, sexual, and creative power. In *The Song of the Lark,* she would make the equivalences among the female body, the pot's shape, and the artist's voice explicit when Thea Kronborg, who also experiences a creative turning point in the Southwest, understands that in singing "one made a vessel of one's throat and nostrils."

Later, Cather liked to view the Southwest as her artistic birthplace; but we can see that it was only the catalyst for creative and psychological processes already underway. She had already begun to explore Nebraska material in her fiction; she had come to the end of her apprenticeship. Cather was ready to receive what the Southwest had to offer, and she returned to New York filled with gifts this trip had given her, gifts that she had in a sense given to herself.

By mid-June, Cather was back with her family in Red Cloud in time for the wheat harvest, a communal activity she had not witnessed in several years. She felt eager to return to her homeland, to "[soak] herself in the scents, the sounds, the colours of Nebraska, the old memories."

Willa and Roscoe Cather converse in his home in Cheyenne, Wyoming. Visiting her family members was not merely a pleasant duty for Willa; the conversations she had and landscapes she saw would trigger her memories and provide inspiration for stories.

This was another successful visit, and she left for the East spiritually and emotionally drenched with her western experiences.

When Cather settled in to Isabelle McClung's house in Pittsburgh in October, ready to begin writing, stories began to emerge that she had not planned. Cather was now able to let go more fully in the creative process and let material emerge from the unconscious. She began a short story set in Nebraska called "The White Mulberry Tree," a tale of tragic love, when all of a sudden it was as if something had exploded inside her: in a flash of enlightenment, "The White Mulberry Tree" entwined itself with "Alexandra," the story Cather had written in Cherry Valley. The two stories belonged together, she realized, and all of a sudden she had a novel on her hands, a novel she had not known she was going to write. After the creative flash in which the stories merged, Cather returned to her craft, developing and connecting them, so when she left Pittsburgh for New York she had a draft of *O Pioneers!* with her.

We can now see how the novel developed from two stories. The dominant narrative is the saga of Alexandra Bergson's taming of the wild Nebraska soil. Inheriting the family farm from her father, she is both a pioneer and an artist like Willa Cather as she learns how to make her native soil bloom. Intertwined with her story is that of her younger brother, Emil, whose love for Marie Shabata, the wife of a neighbor, leads to tragedy. Cather integrates the two stories, however, by showing us they are both tales about passion: Alexandra's passion is directed toward the land, Emil's toward romantic and adulterous love. *O Pioneers!* is also an epic story of the settlement of America. In making the hero of this venture a woman, Cather was rewriting her national myth, which ascribed the creation of culture and the conquering of the frontier to men.

Because this novel and the creative process that produced it were so new, Cather felt both excited and insecure. She told Sergeant that it was the story she had needed and wanted to write, and she had done so as Jewett had recommended—writing without thinking about pleasing anyone but herself. She knew it was good. But then she wondered if anyone else would like it: perhaps no one wanted to read about Nebraska farmers. On the whole, she said, summing up her insecurities, *O Pioneers!* was either pretty good or an utter failure—whatever it was, it was not mediocre.

Cather later realized she had found her own voice in *O Pioneers!* and liked to stress the contrast between her first and her second novel. When she wrote *Alexander's Bridge,* she said, she had been working with material external to her; but in *O Pioneers!* she had drawn on her own "deepest experience," returning to the things she "knew best" and had "[taken] for granted." Sophisticated New York critics might not "care a damn" about Nebraska, but she knew that books like *Alexander's Bridge* were "unnecessary and superfluous" because they were written with such critics in mind; *O Pioneers!* was by contrast "entirely for [her]self." Inscribing a copy of *O Pioneers!* for her Red Cloud friend Carrie Miner Sherwood, Cather wrote: "This was the first time I walked off on my own feet—everything before was half real and half an imitation of writers whom I admired. In this one I hit the home pasture and found I was Yance Sorgeson [a Nebraska farmer] and not Henry James."

In "hitting the home pasture," Cather also tapped into the creative process as many artists describe it. Painters, sculptors, musicians, dancers, and writers often experience heightened states of inspiration in which their material seems to be shaping them, rather than the other way around. Paintings seem to paint themselves, novels to write themselves, characters to take over, as if the artist were a medium for a creative force that flows through him or her on its way toward incarnation on the canvas or the page. Frequently the artist feels a loss of self and of control; the artistic activity then is an act of exploration or journeying rather than a recording of an idea of form that is already present, fully formed, in the artist's mind. After such periods of contact with the unconscious, the artist consciously shapes the material that has been given, relying on craft and intellect. But if an artistic work is to possess the spark of life, many artists believe that such periods of inspiration, in which they feel driven by the unconscious or the muse or some other force larger than the ego, need to occur.

With *O Pioneers!* Cather experienced the creative process in this way. Whereas she had consciously shaped and fashioned *Alexander's Bridge,* *O Pioneers!* "seem[ed] to be there of itself, already moulded." She described the creative intuition to which she had submitted as "the thing by which our feet find the road home on a dark night, accounting of themselves for roots and stones which we had never noticed by day." Another time, she described this process of surrender as "taking a ride through familiar country on a horse that knew the way."

Before riding through familiar country, though, Cather had to tap into unfamiliar country, the emotions and experiences that lay buried inside her. Her true subjects, she realized, arose from her "deepest" feelings, and these did not lie on the surface but were submerged in the "bottom of . . . consciousness." Hence finding the "road home" meant allowing submerged, forgotten, or repressed material to surface. Frequently, Cather's characters gain access to creative force when they allow a connection to an "underground" power: Alexandra Bergson, for example, has an unconscious life that nourishes her crops like an "underground river," and Jim Burden sees Ántonia's maternal power most intensely when she and the children burst out of the fruit cellar at the novel's end.

Cather's "road home" led her to many places besides Nebraska. Novels which drew on her Nebraska past include *O Pioneers!, The Song of the Lark, My Ántonia, One of Ours, A Lost Lady, Lucy Gayheart,* and the short story collection *Obscure Destinies,* which contains "Neighbor Rosicky." But in *The Professor's House* she was drawn to the Southwest; in *Death Comes for the Archbishop* to the missionary experience of Catholic priests in 19th-century New Mexico; in *Shadows on the Rock* to French settlers in 17th-century Quebec; in *Sapphira and the Slave Girl* to 19th-century Virginia. After she found her voice as a novelist, all her fiction—no matter the setting—arose from her deep and passionate response to the world and to her art; all her fiction both created a world separate from herself and drew on her own profound emotions and yearnings. So even though Cather never did write the love story between two women that she might have written had she come of age in the later 20th century, her fiction was authentic, deeply felt, and personal in that it drew on her deepest self.

Adrienne Rich tells us that to be authentic, women's writing must engage in an act of "re-vision"—both rewriting and reseeing. Women writers have inherited many male-authored and patriarchal stories about the world and about women, stories that often deny women creativity and power, such as fairy tales in which the ideal woman waits passively to be awakened by the kiss of Prince Charming. Perhaps because Cather's lesbianism had placed her outside heterosexual and patriarchal stories, she was free when she found her own voice in *O Pioneers!* to revise male-authored stories and to create a different narrative for a woman character than had previously existed in American fiction.

WILLA CATHER

In the works of the major male American authors who preceded Cather, strong, creative women generally ended up punished, diminished, or dead. Think of Hester Prynne in Nathaniel Hawthorne's *The Scarlet Letter,* whose passionate rebellion is chastened into self-sacrificing obedience; or Zenobia in his *Blithedale Romance,* who obligingly drowns herself; or Isabel Archer in Henry James's *The Portrait of a Lady,* who resigns herself to a loveless marriage; or Carrie in Theodore Dreiser's *Sister Carrie,* who ends the novel rocking, rocking, staring into space; or Charlotte Stant in James's *Golden Bowl,* who numbly accepts exile in the provincial wastes of America.

And if we look at the fiction by women writers who preceded Cather, we generally see a similar pattern, as if women did not have the power to challenge male-authored stories. Female characters who end happily in the novels by sentimental and domestic writers who dominated the 19th-century literary marketplace generally follow the love-and-marriage plot, frequently sacrificing artistic abilities for the sake of husbands and children. Kate Chopin did challenge this plot in *The Awakening,* but her revision was not an optimistic one: the rebellious Edna Pontellier, who seeks creative self-discovery, can find no space for herself in a culture that defines motherhood as woman's destiny and walks into the Gulf of Mexico at the novel's end.

Another pattern Cather inherited from the major male writers of the 19th century that also needed revising was the absence of women from literature. In the fictional worlds of James Fenimore Cooper, Nathaniel Hawthorne, Mark Twain, Herman Melville, and Henry David Thoreau, all important human activity was carried out by men, frequently male friends or comrades whose bond made women extraneous (Natty Bumppo and Chingachgook in *The Last of the Mohicans,* Huck and Jim in *Huckleberry Finn,* Ishmael and Queequeg in the all-male *Moby Dick*).

So the fates for women characters Willa Cather inherited from 19th-century American fiction—marriage, punishment, death, or absence—were hardly models she wanted to emulate. Thus, in *O Pioneers!* she broke new fictional ground when she created Alexandra Bergson, a strong pioneer farm woman who integrates conventionally masculine

EVERY ARTIST MAKES HERSELF BORN

and feminine qualities without being male-identified. In Alexandra, Cather gives us a model of female strength that reflects her own move from male identification to acceptance of her womanhood, a womanhood separated from the dominant culture's definition of the feminine as submissive and domestic.

In the first few pages, we see Alexandra wearing a "man's long ulster," which she carries comfortably, like a "young soldier." Yet if we now assume she is mannish, Cather confuses us when the "young soldier" takes off her veil to reveal a sign of female beauty, a "shining mass of hair . . . two thick braids, pinned about her head in the German

Cather's first cousin, Grosvenor P. Cather, poses with his wife in this portrait taken shortly before his death in World War I. Grosvenor was the model for Claude, the Nebraskan hero of *One of Ours,* the novel for which Cather won the 1923 Pulitzer Prize.

way, with a fringe of reddish-yellow curls." Later, Cather grants the older Alexandra a physical presence that is not conventionally feminine. She is not seductive or delicate or self-conscious about her appearance but is still powerfully female. "Sunnier" and "more vigorous" than she was as a girl, the older Alexandra still has the beautiful "fiery" hair that makes her resemble a sunflower. Her face is always tanned in the summer from her work outside, but when her collar falls away from her neck or she pushes up her sleeves, we can see that her skin has the "smoothness and whiteness as none but Swedish women ever possess; skin with the freshness of the snow itself."

We can see the same contradictory qualities in Alexandra throughout the novel: she is a strong but not mannish woman, and her relationship to the land shows her possessing human qualities that Cather's culture wanted to section off between men and women. Assertive, farseeing, risk taking, Alexandra rules the farm and her brothers with the authority that most American writers would have assigned to heroes. But unlike the men in the novel, she does not want to subdue or dominate the soil in an aggressive, antagonistic way. Alexandra finally succeeds as a farmer because of her passion and love for a seemingly barren landscape and her maternal desire to nurture. She can see the land's beauty and fertility where others see only drought and suffering. Because she freely gives her love to the soil, Cather suggests, the spirit of the soil, like a lover, responds and allows her to make the land bloom.

O Pioneers! was a bold achievement for a second novel. Not only did Cather return to her own material and write in her own voice, but she also rewrote the conventional gender plots she had inherited from both male and female writers, giving her heroine a destiny in which creativity and companionship could be combined.

Cather's editor at Houghton Mifflin, Ferris Greenslet, was impressed with the novel and told his colleagues it would establish Cather as "novelist of the first rank." Most reviewers agreed, praising her use of American materials and settings. Some even applauded her creation of a strong, unorthodox heroine in Alexandra. The reviewer for the *New York Times* thought Cather had created a "new mythology" by replacing the traditional American hero with a woman who possesses a "deep instinct for the land" and for lives lived close to the soil. This was a "feminine" story, the reviewer concluded, and yet it was also "American in the best sense of the word," describing as it did the American story of emigration and settlement. Cather also received a glowing notice from the Lincoln *Sunday State Journal;* it must have pleased her to read a hometown review that called her novel "extraordinary" and "beautiful."

Willa Cather never returned permanently to the staff of *McClure's*. After *O Pioneers!* was published, she wrote freelance articles for the magazine and took on the paradoxical job of ghostwriting S. S. McClure's autobiography. It appeared in the magazine under his name, with only the acknowledgment, "I wish to express my indebtedness to Miss Willa Sibert Cather for her invaluable assistance in the preparation of these memoirs." This would be the last time Cather would publish something for which she did not receive full recognition. But doubtless doing McClure this favor helped her to ease her departure from the magazine.

One of Cather's freelance articles, "Three American Singers," had a profound impact on her next novel, *The Song of the Lark*. Cather had long been interested in opera and considered the divas who dominated the stage the epitome of the woman-as-artist. For her article, she chose to interview three of America's most famous women opera singers: Louise Homer, Geraldine Farrar, and Olive Fremstad, a Swedish-born immigrant who had, like Cather, grown up in the Midwest. Cather and Fremstad became friends, and the singer helped the writer to imagine the character of Thea Kronborg.

Had Cather met Fremstad a few years earlier, during the period when she felt drained and insecure, she might have felt intimidated by the singer's success and self-assurance. But as it was, Cather was ready for a more equal friendship. She could sense the analogy between her own transition from the short story to the novel and Fremstad's courageous decision to extend her vocal range from contralto to soprano—preparing herself to take on opera's most central and dramatic female roles. Singing teachers, music critics, and operagoers had all agreed that Fremstad's strength was in her lower tones, but she believed that the "Swedish voice is always long," and so she extended her upper scale "tone by tone, without much encouragement." "I do not claim this or that for my voice," Fremstad told Cather. "I do not sing contralto or soprano. I sing Isolde. What voice is necessary for the part I undertake, I will produce."

As the author of *O Pioneers!* who had also produced the voice she needed for the part, Cather delighted in the correspondences she saw between herself and Fremstad, as well as the similarities between Fremstad and the strong immigrant women on the Divide. In *The Song of the Lark,* we see the stories of Cather and Fremstad combined in Thea, the singer who discovers the power of her voice after a liberating sojourn in the Southwest. The strongest autobiographical source for the novel, however, was the emergence of her own writer's voice in *O Pioneers!* Cather could not have written *The Song of the Lark* if she were not sure she, too, was an artist.

The letters Cather sent to Ferris Greenslet while she was writing *The Song of the Lark* exude self-confidence and excitement. She told him she liked her latest novel better than *O Pioneers!* and enjoyed writing it more as well. She dared to say she thought he would not publish a story like it every day.

There were many reasons for Cather's self-assured delight in her new novel: her exhilarating friendship with Fremstad; her success with *O Pioneers!;* her unleashing of pent-up creative energies; her recognition that she, like the opera singers she admired, possessed a distinctive voice. Underlying these was her new freedom to tell, if she wished, the story of a woman's power and achievement. She knew she had done this in *The Song of the Lark:* she told Greenslet that Houghton Mifflin should be sure to advertise the novel at women's colleges. Students at Smith, Barnard, and Radcliffe would like Thea, she knew; they wanted a model of defiant, unsentimental success.

When Cather dedicated *The Song of the Lark* to Isabelle and her "garden fair," she acknowledged her friend's power to create a blessed, protected space filled with growth, blooming, and beauty. But shortly after *The Song of the Lark* was published, Cather had to leave her garden fair. Isabelle's father died in 1915, and the Pittsburgh house was sold,

EVERY ARTIST MAKES HERSELF BORN

so Cather lost both a home and a creative sanctuary. She liked her Bank Street apartment, she told a friend, but it did not seem like home in the way Isabelle's house did, able to make her feel safe and happy.

Then, a few months later, came even more terrible news: Isabelle announced her upcoming marriage to violinist Jan Hambourg. Cather at first was devastated by this apparently unexpected turn of events. Writing to her friend Dorothy Canfield, she said that the change in her life was irrevocable, the loss overwhelming. When she talked with Elizabeth Sergeant about Isabelle's marriage, her eyes were "vacant," her face "bleak." "All her natural exuberance had drained away," Sergeant remembered. Cather did not know how, or if, she could survive this loss.

The winter of 1915–16 was grim, filled with the "loss of old friends by death and even by marriage," as Cather admitted to a friend. Indeed, marriage for her was a kind of death, taking Isabelle away from her permanently. Throughout the winter and spring, Cather remained grieving and depressed. She had an idea for a new novel—a novel that would be *My Ántonia*—but she had no interest or desire to begin it. Her creative force seemed as empty as Nebraska's winter landscape would to Jim Burden.

But Cather was resilient in both her life and her art, and the renewal in life preceded the renewal in her writing. In the summer of 1916, she traveled west, staying in New Mexico—always a landscape of rebirth for her—and visiting her brother Roscoe in Wyoming. She was having a wonderful time, she wrote to Sergeant: Isabelle's marriage was still hard and always would be, but the rest of the world was still there. Then Cather returned to Red Cloud for several months, feeling she had left the dark winter of her soul behind in the Rockies. While in Red Cloud, she visited family and old friends and renewed a friendship with a Bohemian woman, Annie Sadilek Pavelka, whom she had known in childhood as one of the immigrant "hired girls" who worked for native-born families.

When Cather returned to New York in November 1916, *My Ántonia* was ready to emerge, and she wrote steadily and well for several months. Simultaneously, she was coming to accept, as was necessary, Isabelle's marriage. Isabelle and Jan Hambourg were living in New York, and Cather exchanged dinner invitations with them.

Eventually, Isabelle and Jan would move to France. The love between the two women persisted, maintained through letters and visits, and Cather retained Isabelle as beloved friend, reader, and muse. Isabelle's letters to Cather reveal the deep affection she always held for her friend, as we can see from their salutations and closings: "My darling Willa," "Darling Willa," "So lovingly to you, Isabelle," "A loving heart to you, I.," "So lovingly, Isabelle."

But after her marriage, Isabelle was no longer as available to Cather as she had been, and Cather compensated for this loss by sharing more of her life with Edith Lewis. Now that Cather was no longer leaving New York for long stays in Pittsburgh, she and Lewis began to develop their own social life as a couple, hosting Friday afternoon open houses at their Bank Street apartment. New York friends, Greenwich Village neighbors, artists, writers, publishers, visitors from Nebraska, journalists passing through town—an interesting and ever-changing group of people would come to Cather's apartment for tea and conversation. "Those informal gatherings around the coal fire in the living-room at 5 Bank Street, with the late winter sunshine slowly changing into dusk, and the melodious sound of the tugboat whistles coming up from the river nearby, were very pleasant," remembered Edith Lewis. "Everyone talked as if there was not nearly enough time for all they had to say. Often a small group of Willa Cather's more intimate friends would stay on after the others had drifted away, lingering until eight o'clock or later." So Isabelle's loss brought Cather a gain: she was beginning to make Bank Street her home, and so, in a sense, to become more integrated. Gradually, Bank Street would become the creative sanctuary she shaped herself, with Edith Lewis's help. Pittsburgh was gone, but now, in her own home, she could write.

Cather's creativity was still supported by a combination of rootedness and travel. Now that Bank Street was the home of her writing, she found another away-from-home retreat in which to work: the Shattuck Inn in Jaffrey, New Hampshire, near Mount Monadnock. She rented two rooms on the top floor. "They had sloping ceilings," Lewis recalled,

EVERY ARTIST MAKES HERSELF BORN

"like her attic room in the old days in Red Cloud, and on the roof directly overhead she could hear the rain in wet weather." Cather stayed there for two months in the fall of 1917. Friends from Pittsburgh had rented a nearby cottage and put a tent up in their meadow where Cather could write. So every morning she set off for her outdoor studio, a half-mile walk through the woods that prepared her soul for writing. She worked for a few hours on *My Ántonia* and then spent the afternoons hiking, the evenings socializing.

Cather returned to Jaffrey in the fall for several years, often accompanied by Lewis. The wooded natural setting—so different from Nebraska, so similar to Virginia—helped give Cather distance from the powerful emotional material from her past, Lewis thought. Surrounded by the tranquil beauty of a New England fall, Cather could safely draw on the potent sources of her art. "The fresh, pine-scented woods and pastures," said Lewis, "with their multitudinous wild flowers, the gentle

The Miner home in Red Cloud, Nebraska, one block west of Cather's childhood home.
The house became the setting for much of Cather's *My Ántonia,* and the Miners themselves were transformed in the novel into the Harling family.

skies, the little enclosed fields, had in them nothing of the disturbing, exalting, impelling memories and associations of the past—her own past. Every day there was like an empty canvas, a clean sheet of paper to be filled. She lived with a simple sense of physical well-being, of weather, and of country solitude."

Solitude, but not loneliness. In Jaffrey, as in New York, Cather could have companionship when she needed it: friends, other guests at the inn, and Edith Lewis, who generally came for part of Cather's stay. So in the summer of 1918, Cather read proofs for *My Ántonia*—a potentially lonely job—with Edith in the woods near the Shattuck Inn. "These were wonderful mornings," Lewis wrote, "full of beauty and pleasure."

My Ántonia was the most daring novel Willa Cather had yet written. In returning to memories of her childhood and youth in Nebraska, she crafted a novel that was experimental in both form and content. *My Ántonia* is a drama of memory. Narrated by Jim Burden, the novel tells the story of Ántonia Shimerda, the Bohemian immigrant girl who preoccupies Jim's imagination throughout his life. The character of Ántonia is based on Annie Sadilek, a childhood friend of Cather's.

Retrospectively narrated—Jim is in midlife—the novel evokes the intensity of his frontier childhood and of Ántonia's vitality, but always with a sense of loss, for we feel that Jim has not found fulfillment in his adult life. Because, according to Cather's narrative method, Jim not only tells but also *writes* the story we read, we also sense that for Jim, as for Cather, loss is a spark for creativity. He makes the past come to life by transforming remembered experience into language.

Like memory, which is a collection of separate and sometimes unconnected images, *My Ántonia* is told through vignettes (sometimes widely separated in time), inset stories, and word pictures that, taken together, make up a photograph album of the past. There is no conventional love story, no linear dramatic action, no single conflict and resolution. But if readers of the novel give up their expectations for a conventionally plotted story, they find in *My Ántonia* a beautifully crafted, lyrical evocation of the American past—and of the universal experience of childhood, as remembered in adult life.

EVERY ARTIST MAKES HERSELF BORN

"Life began for me," Cather once said, "when I ceased to admire and began to remember," and certainly *My Ántonia* reveals the mingling of memory and imagination that gave rise to Cather's greatest fiction. She dedicated the novel to her longtime Red Cloud friends Carrie and Irene Miner—"In memory of affections old and true"—and Cather's remembered affections for old and true friends colored many of her fictional portraits. Carrie Miner becomes Frances Harling, Mrs. Miner is Mrs. Harling (the only exact fictional portrait Cather claims to have drawn), and, most centrally, the Bohemian "hired girl" Annie Sadilek becomes Ántonia Shimerda, the figure who represents to Cather and to her narrator Jim Burden "the country, the conditions, the whole adventure of our childhood." In creating Jim, Cather drew on the curve of her own life—the move from Virginia to Nebraska, the youth spent in a provincial small town, the college years at the University of Nebraska, the eastern professional success, and the memory and emotions that keep returning, time after time, to the past.

Because of the beautiful simplicity of the novel's prose, and because there did not seem to be unsuitable violent or sexual material in the novel, *My Ántonia* has been thought appropriate for young readers and is traditionally read in high schools. Indeed, there are beautiful, poetic descriptions of landscape and farming in *My Ántonia,* but there is also violence and sex aplenty: the suicide of Mr. Shimerda; the bride fed to the wolves; Wick Cutter's attempted rape of Jim (posing as Ántonia); Ántonia's seduction and "disgrace" as an unwed mother; Jim's erotic (and perhaps masochistic) fantasy of Lena with a "curved reaping hook," telling him, "Now they are all gone, and I can kiss you as much as I like"; Jim's dalliance with Lena in Lincoln; and, winding its way through the novel, the sexual and erotic allure of the working-class "hired girls" who distract Red Cloud's middle-class young men.

While early readings of the novel tended to view it as an elegiac, nostalgic narrative of the frontier, later readings have taken account of the darker, more disturbing material. Some critics see sexual fear underlying the novel, pointing to the fact that Jim, although preoccupied with Ántonia and Lena, never achieves a satisfactory sexual and emotional relationship with either one, and is, as far as we know,

WILLA CATHER

Annie Sadilek, a Czech immigrant who worked for a native-born family in Red Cloud, Nebraska, during Cather's childhood, was a lifelong friend of Cather's and the inspiration for the character of Ántonia.

unhappily married. Other readers see the novel as a feminist critique of male-authored stories and myths, pointing to Jim's somewhat reductive and certainly patriarchal view of Ántonia as a maternal earth mother: a "rich mine of life" who produced "sons that stood tall and straight," a vision that not only defines Ántonia solely by her fertility but also leaves out her daughters. Still other readers see Cather as perpetuating, rather than challenging, limiting male representations of women. And others regard her as the lesbian writer who used Jim as an unconvincing mask for her own "unnatural" love for women.

My Ántonia has increasingly attracted complex and often contradictory interpretations because of its unusual narrative structure. In contrast to *O Pioneers!* and *The Song of the Lark*, *My Ántonia* has a first-person narrator, Jim Burden. Cather explained her switch from the third-person omniscient narration she employed in the other two novels by saying that novels of action were best told in the third person, but novels of feeling, like *My Ántonia*, were best told in the first person.

EVERY ARTIST MAKES HERSELF BORN

Because Cather gave some of her own experiences to Jim, some critics believe she is identified with him, and that his opinions are also hers. But other critics, reminding us that there is a difference between life and fiction and author and character, argue that Cather retains an ironic distance from Jim, and so we should not confuse his views of the world with hers.

My own view is that Cather wavers in this narrative: at times, she seems merged with Jim; at other times, she is the separate author self-consciously working with a fictional character. This complex relationship between author and narrative gives us a novel that is rich with ambiguity, a novel that can yield no simple or unified interpretation.

Jim and Cather are most similar—in addition to the biographical details—in the sources of their creativity. Both are writers and storytellers, and both find loss, change, and memory central to their creative process. We need to remember that Jim does not merely narrate the story, as Nick Carraway does *The Great Gatsby:* according to the fictional device Cather creates in her introduction, Jim actually *writes* the story we read. And the source of his narrative is the desire to recapture, in writing, experiences, friendships, and moments that are far in the past, retained only in memory. "Some memories are better than anything that will happen to you again," Jim says, and the tone of melancholy longing in that comment suggests how important loss is to his creative process: loss in fact sparks his writing. Although Jim has a life of many losses—he has a loveless marriage, he is childless, he locates the happiest days of his life in the past—in writing the past comes alive for him. He tells us this several times: "I can remember exactly how the country looked to me," "All the years that have passed have not dimmed my memory of that first glorious autumn," and phrases such as "I can see them now" or "They are with me still" recur throughout the novel. "They were so much alive in me," Jim says, speaking of the memories of Black Hawk friends he brings with him when he leaves for Lincoln, "that I scarcely stopped to wonder whether they were alive anywhere else, or how."

Loss was also central to Willa Cather's creativity. She needed the separation—and the sadness—that time and distance brought from the emotions of her past and from people she had loved or desired. The creative act of writing, although having its roots in loss, then brought compensation and renewal as Cather, like Jim, could bring a world she had lost to life on the page. Many of her novels, like *My Ántonia*, were sparked by her yearning and desire to recapture figures from the past, either her own past or the historical past.

Writing also brought compensation for the losses and absences that accompanied Cather throughout her life. The loss of Isabelle directly preceded the writing of *My Ántonia;* having lost one maternal presence in her life, by going back to the figure of Ántonia, Cather could recreate another maternal presence in her art.

We can see this intertwining of loss and gain in the novel Cather wrote: to accept life, *My Ántonia* suggests, is also to accept loss and change. Jim Burden observes that late fall afternoons are the most beautiful time of day: when the "haystacks turned rosy and threw long shadows . . . it was a sudden transfiguration, a lifting-up of day." The late afternoon sun is about to sink and autumn will move into winter, as the image of the long shadows reminds us. And yet the cycle of the seasons holds out hope for renewal: as Percy Bysshe Shelley asked in "Ode to the West Wind," "If winter come, can spring be far behind?"

Ántonia, who becomes for Jim the symbol of the life force, suffers the loss of her beloved father, the loss of her lover, the loss of her reputation, the loss of her youth. But these losses are intertwined with the images of powerful growth and life we see in "Cuzak's Boys," the novel's last section: Ántonia's children bursting out of the fruit cellar, the protected orchard holding the sun "like a cup," Ántonia's box of photographs, pictures of the frozen past that come to life when she tells Jim the stories that go with them.

Perhaps because *My Ántonia,* Cather's novel of feeling, juxtaposed loss and creativity more poignantly for her than did her earlier novels, she remained particularly protective of the novel after its publication, watching out for *My Ántonia*'s health and safety as a mother would care for a child. In her letters to Ferris Greenslet, her editor, Cather always referred to her novel as "she" or "her"—suggesting that she identified

EVERY ARTIST MAKES HERSELF BORN

Cather operates a handcar during a vacation in Wyoming. Her descriptions of the open western landscape in her fiction are famous for their expansive, mysterious quality.

the novel with Ántonia and perhaps with herself. She fought fiercely to keep *My Ántonia* out of the movies and out of paperback. Either form of publication would cheapen her work, she believed, as well as removing it from her maternal control. Ántonia had done well enough for her publisher "as she is," Cather told Greenslet sternly in the 1940s, and neither she nor Ántonia wanted to be in a cut-rate drugstore or railway station along with other paperbacks.

Most reviews of *My Ántonia* were glowing. Cather had come of age as a novelist, reviewers felt, and could now be counted among the first rank of American writers. H. L. Mencken, editor of the important magazine *Smart Set* and one of America's foremost critics, told his readers that *My Ántonia* was not only Cather's best novel, it was also "one of the best that any American has ever done." Many contemporary readers and critics would agree with Mencken, and if Cather had stopped writing with *My Ántonia,* she would still be considered one of our finest writers. But an extraordinarily productive literary career lay ahead of her as Cather continued to grow and deepen as a woman and as a writer.

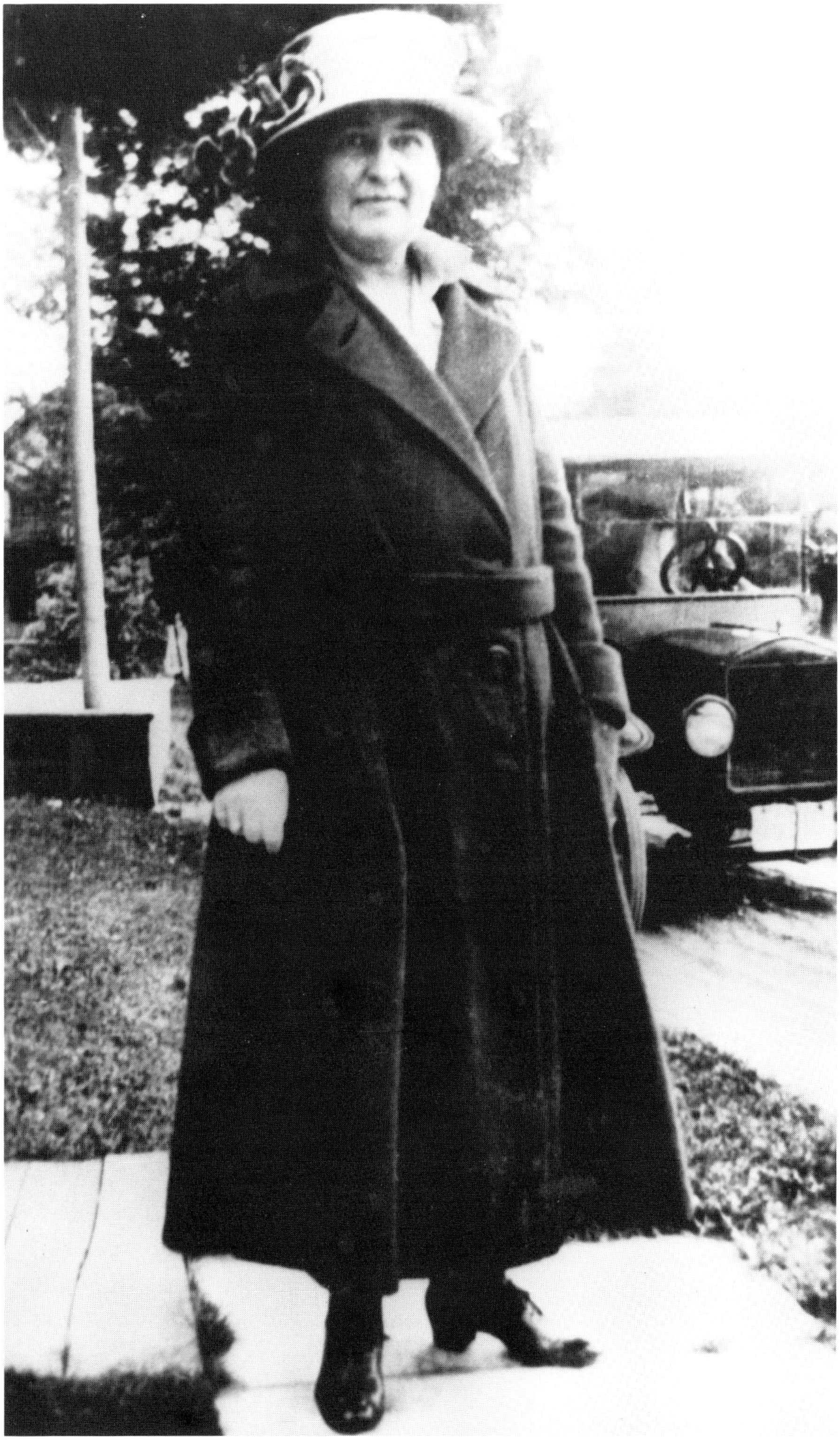

CHAPTER SIX

THE WRITING LIFE

Cather waits outside the Writers School in Bread Loaf, Vermont. Although some later readers were critical of her choice of subject matter in her novels and stories, Cather's ability as a writer has always been highly esteemed.

Following the successes of *O Pioneers!, The Song of the Lark,* and *My Ántonia,* three powerful novels written within a six-year period, we might fear that a dry spell awaited Willa Cather, or perhaps a declining curve of literary production and excellence. After all, some of the best American writers—Ralph Ellison, J. D. Salinger, Henry Roth—publish only one or two books and then fall silent for years, perhaps forever. "There are no second acts in American lives," commented F. Scott Fitzgerald. Fitzgerald, who had trouble moving on from his masterwork, *The Great Gatsby,* was referring to the tendency of American artists to flame early and brilliantly and then burn out.

But Willa Cather's creative fire glowed for almost three more decades after the publication of *My Ántonia,* at times burning higher when she produced a novel such as *Death Comes for the Archbishop* (which won great acclaim), but always steadily. *Youth and the Bright Medusa,* a collection of stories, was published in 1920; the novel *One of Ours* in 1922; the novel *A Lost*

WILLA CATHER

Lady in 1923; the novel *The Professor's House* in 1925; the novella *My Mortal Enemy* in 1926; the novel *Death Comes for the Archbishop* in 1927; the novel *Shadows on the Rock* in 1931; the short story collection *Obscure Destinies* in 1932; the novel *Lucy Gayheart* in 1935; the essay collection *Not Under Forty* in 1936; the novel *Sapphira and the Slave Girl* in 1940; a posthumous collection of stories in 1948 (*The Old Beauty and Others*); and one of essays in 1949 (*Willa Cather on Writing*).

So between 1918 and 1940, a 22-year period, Cather published 11 works of fiction or nonfiction, roughly a publication every two years. This is an extraordinary pattern of productivity, particularly when we consider the literary excellence of her writing. During these years, Cather was increasingly praised as one of America's finest novelists, and her work won respectful and enthusiastic reviews from major newspapers and periodicals such as the *New York Times,* the *New Republic,* and the *Nation.* She won the Pulitzer Prize for *One of Ours,* her war novel, and gathered several other honors and awards over her long literary career. Moreover, her books sold well—her fiction was loved by the general reader as well as honored by the critic.

Many novelists who have been as gifted did not match Cather's literary output. How did she manage to keep her creative forces flowing so steadily for so many years? She did not simply rely on serendipitous visits from the muse: she was unusually effective at marshaling the practical and emotional resources she needed to write and to publish.

Perhaps Cather's most strategic move was her decision to change publishers, moving from Houghton Mifflin to Alfred A. Knopf's publishing company after *My Ántonia* was published. At first, she had been thrilled to be publishing with Houghton Mifflin; but as she became more assured of her literary power, and as positive reviews accumulated, she became dissatisfied with Houghton Mifflin on a number of counts. Like many authors, she felt that her publishers were not devoting enough time, attention, and money to her cause: they were not advertising her novels strongly or well; they were not distributing review copies widely enough; they were not keeping bookstores stocked with copies. Cather also wanted more control over the aesthetics of book design—binding, paper, printing, cover—than Houghton

THE WRITING LIFE

Mifflin allowed. In one letter to her editor, Ferris Greenslet, she asked him if something could not be done about the dreadful mud-colored binding for *My Ántonia* in a second edition.

Cather's determination to control the aesthetic shape of the text as a whole reached a height with *My Ántonia,* when she personally commissioned line-drawing illustrations from artist W. T. Benda. When her publisher then balked at paying, she found herself increasingly frustrated by Houghton Mifflin's stinginess and aesthetic shortsightedness. And when Houghton Mifflin, in her view, charged her excessively for corrections she made to page proofs for *My Ántonia,* she wrote Greenslet a long, irritated letter detailing her various complaints. All in all, she told him, she felt that Houghton Mifflin simply did not believe sufficiently in her and her work. "Frankly I despair of any future with [Houghton Mifflin]," she told him.

The stage was set for the most significant move Cather would make in her literary career: her decision to choose Alfred A. Knopf as her publisher, which she did in 1920. Alfred Knopf had recently founded a small publishing company devoted to publishing the finest European

This illustration from the 1918 edition of *My Ántonia* by W. T. Benda shows a buxom Ántonia knitting barefoot on the plain. Ántonia's robustness is characteristic of Cather's heroines; she frequently combined "masculine" physical strength with "feminine" beauty and activities in her female characters.

and American writers and to uniting literary excellence, high-quality book design, and commercial success. "We'll take any amount of pains with a book," he told Cather, and she knew she would find the kind of individual, respectful attention for herself and her work she had not found at Houghton Mifflin. And she must have been flattered to join a publisher whose list included the German novelist Thomas Mann and New Zealand–born short story writer Katherine Mansfield.

Knopf valued Cather's writing and wanted to put his aesthetic and financial resources behind it, and he wooed her by offering to reprint *The Troll Garden*. In 1920, he published the short story collection *Youth and the Bright Medusa,* which contained some reprinted stories from *The Troll Garden* and some new works. Cather was so pleased by Knopf's attention to aesthetic detail and by his commitment to advertising and promotion that she decided to make the move permanent.

It would be a happy and mutually beneficial relationship. As Edith Lewis observed, "Next to writing her novels, Willa Cather's choice of Alfred Knopf influenced her career, I think, more than any action she ever took. It was not so much that with him she was able in a few years to achieve financial security . . . as that he gave her great encouragement and absolute liberty to write exactly as she chose—protected her in every way he could from outside pressures and interruptions—and made evident, not only to her but to the world in general, his great admiration and belief in her."

In Alfred Knopf, Willa Cather found the ideal combination, a publisher who supported her artistic integrity and made money for her at the same time. Thus, she could reconcile the two seemingly contradictory values of art and economics; she could devote herself to the creative process without thinking of sales, and at the same time find enough royalties flowing in to make her a rich woman. She made $19,000 during her third year with Knopf, a substantial sum in 1923. And despite Lewis's disclaimer, Cather did not scorn money: she liked to live comfortably.

Cather's literary career combined artistic integrity with savvy professionalism as she continued to manage the author's role with surety and aplomb. Not only did she find a publisher who could promote her

THE WRITING LIFE

work both aesthetically and financially, but she also made good use of a new figure on the American publishing scene: the literary agent. Paul Reynolds made a good deal of money for Cather by placing her stories and novels in magazines, for example selling the serial rights to *The Professor's House* to *Collier's* for $10,000. Cather seems to have not enjoyed meeting with her agent—Reynolds's letters to her are filled with plaintive requests that the two meet, if only on a bench in Central Park for a chat—but he was a necessary go-between for her, bridging the world of art and the world of money, two realms that, according to American ideology, are not supposed to coexist.

With the aid of Reynolds as well as Knopf, Cather thus carried off the possibly uneasy alliance between creativity and commercial success. Fond of good food, good wine, travel, and tasteful furnishings, she did

Playwright Zoë Akins met Cather through *McClure's* magazine, when Cather rejected some of her poetry. Cather suggested that Akins try writing plays and became a mentor for Akins later in her life, although Cather also relied on Akins as a critic.

not want to have to choose between art and affluence—and luckily for her, she did not have to.

Cather also created the right conditions for writing by surrounding herself with friends who supported her creativity. She needed both solitude and intimacy in order to write, and she found friends who gave her both. Isabelle McClung and Elizabeth Sergeant were the key figures in Cather's early writing life, while Dorothy Canfield Fisher and Zoë Akins were the friends of Cather's middle and late career. And Edith Lewis was Cather's continuing source of creative and emotional support, sharing in the dailiness of Cather's writing life.

According to Lewis, Cather found writing a joyous process because she was never sure when she sat down at her writing desk exactly where a story would take her: "When she began a novel she began it, I think, as someone might begin a journey. She knew her direction and her destination, and some of the places she might visit on the way; but she never carefully plotted out beforehand the actual journey itself . . . I think this would have spoiled all her pleasure in writing. And to her, writing was an intense and, I believe, an unmixed pleasure."

Writing for Cather was an act of exploration and discovery; she had to write in order to find out what she was going to say. As she wrote, characters would come alive and live out destinies she might not have planned for them on the page. "The journey, not the arrival matters," Cather was fond of quoting, and she succeeded as a writer paradoxically because she enjoyed the process rather than hurrying to get to the product. "It was this activity of creating the thing as she wrote that she enjoyed," Lewis remembered, "as one might enjoy a fast game of tennis." Writing for her was more a form of play than work: Elizabeth Sergeant remembered arriving at Bank Street one day, when Cather was still at the typewriter, and seeing her friend jump up to greet her with "a face of bliss, like a child's."

Because Cather was allowing a spontaneous process of discovery to take place, she always wrote her first drafts rapidly—and by hand. The intimate connection between her hand, the pen, and the page was important to her; because her writing was so self-expressive, she must have felt that the technology of the typewriter would intervene between

THE WRITING LIFE

herself and the flow of words. When she had a first draft, she would turn to the typewriter and rewrite, often revising several pages as she kept one eye on her handwritten text.

Then Cather made use of another practical writer's aid: a secretary. Given a clean copy, Cather would revise the manuscript again—maybe several times—but there was always her secretary (quite an asset in the era before word processors and Xerox machines) to give her a freshly typed and corrected version. When she received galley and page proofs from Knopf, Cather would make still more alterations. Sometimes, when a novel went into a second edition, she would make substantial changes, as in the case of *O Pioneers!*, *The Song of the Lark,* and *My Ántonia*.

Perhaps because Cather found writing a form of recreation rather than achievement, she was able to balance her writing with many other of life's pleasures. Generally, she would only work in the mornings, writing for two or three hours. Then there would be a hearty lunch (she liked to eat) cooked and served by Josephine Bourda, Cather's French housekeeper during the Bank Street years and, according to Lewis, a "splendid cook." The afternoons generally involved outdoor excursions—Cather loved walking, weather, and physical exercise. "Rapid motion was essential to her," Sergeant wrote: Cather needed to "dissolve into nature daily in order to be reborn to a task."

While Cather's daily rhythms included walks and hikes through the restorative natural world (Central Park while she was in New York), her yearly rhythms included travel to the landscapes she loved: Nebraska, the Southwest, Wyoming, New England. When she traveled west, Cather devoted herself to family and friends, storing up impressions for later writing. As soon as she had returned east, with a safe distance from her past, she could turn memory and emotion into art.

Cather loved her summer and fall retreat, the Shattuck Inn in Jaffrey, where she wrote *My Ántonia*. During the 1920s, she had a cabin built on the island of Grand Manan, a few miles off the coast of New Brunswick. There she could combine many of her pleasures: vacation, nature, writing, travel, food and drink (because Grand Manan was a Canadian possession, Cather could have wine shipped there while the

United States went dry under Prohibition). There she could have "solitude without loneliness," Lewis recalled, writing in a large attic room overlooking the Atlantic Ocean. The cabin space echoed the other attic rooms where she loved to write—in the Shattuck Inn, at Isabelle's house—which recalled her childhood bedroom in Red Cloud.

Some viewers of Cather's life see her as a lonely, almost isolated artist, particularly in the second half of her life. It is true that in later years she more and more valued her privacy, preferring to spend time only with her oldest and closest friends. The poet Robert Frost, referring to Cather's aloofness, reportedly said, "With Carl Sandburg it's the people, yes; with Willa Cather, it's the people, no." Cather seemed more and more withdrawn to Elizabeth Sergeant, whose memoir described the older Cather as guarded and remote. Given Cather's partnership with Edith Lewis and her many friendships with women, she was not isolated. But increasingly she chose to protect her creativity by avoiding people who drained her energy and spending time only with people who counted emotionally, which may have been why some observers thought her isolated. She maintained close ties with her old friends and family, particularly her brothers Roscoe and Douglass, and although she withdrew from an active social life, she remained open to new and enriching attachments throughout her life.

During the 1930s and 1940s, Cather developed a number of relationships with younger people, finding emotional satisfaction as she grew older in being an aunt and a maternal friend. She was close to her nieces and nephews, frequently inviting her nieces to stay with her on Grand Manan and in New York. She became friends with the Menuhin family; the European-born father was a violinist, and all three children—Hephzibah, Yaltah, and Yehudi—were musically gifted. (Ultimately, Yehudi Menuhin would surpass his father as a violinist, becoming known as the greatest virtuoso of his time.) Cather spent "unclouded time" with the Menuhin children, Edith Lewis remembered; she would take them on walks to Central Park and excursions to the opera; she read Shakespeare to them; she shared their holidays and birthdays. The Menuhin children in turn worshiped the woman they called Aunt Willa as their "greatest hero." "One could tell her

THE WRITING LIFE

Thanks to the financial and critical success of novels such as *O Pioneers!* and *My Ántonia*, Cather was free to travel and meet other well-known artists. Here she visits painter Léon Bakst at his studio in Paris, France.

everything in one's heart," Yehudi Menuhin recalled; "it would never be used, never turned against one, never cause her to alter her regard." Cather did display a "contempt" for anything "determined by mobs," he thought, and she withdrew "more and more from society even as she drew closer to us."

During the 1930s, Cather also developed an unusual friendship with a young British aristocrat, dilettante, writer, and homosexual named Stephan Tennant. She found him outrageous, charming, and playful, and gave him literary advice and professional guidance which Tennant seems not to have followed. But his admiration was flattering to her, and she may well have seen something of herself—of her old William Cather identity—in Tennant's effeminate flamboyance. In a way, he was her opposite and her double, crossing the gender boundary from the other direction.

Some of Cather's biographers, such as Elizabeth Sergeant, may not have seen how many relationships flowed into Cather's creativity because their vision was shaped by an aesthetic ideology we have inherited from the Romantics that tells us artists are sensitive, lonely souls separated somehow from the common, vulgar mass of humanity. Our exalted ideas about artists seem to require they suffer the rigors of loneliness in order to create. Somehow, we don't think artistic greatness can reside in a mere mortal human being who maintains an extensive correspondence, lunches with her publisher, visits her family, takes children to the opera, and has wine shipped to New Brunswick.

But these are false assumptions, and Cather's life story reminds us of how important a balanced emotional and professional life is to a creative spirit. Cather's steady rate of publication throughout the 1920s and 1930s seems more understandable when we think of all the different relationships—with her publisher, agent, cook-housekeeper, secretary, partner, friends, fellow writers, parents, brothers and sisters, nieces and nephews, younger acquaintances—that helped to nurture her personally and professionally. These relationships were particularly important when Cather lost the stability of her Bank Street home: she had to move in 1927 because her building was being torn down. For almost five years, Cather and Edith Lewis made a temporary home at the Grosvenor Hotel, finally moving to another apartment on Park Avenue.

Another form of relationship sustained Willa Cather while she was writing—that with her characters. Many of her novels were inspired by remembered or imagined relationships, so creating a character was a way of connecting to someone from her past. And once that character took on a life of his or her own, Cather found fiction writing was a form of relationship with a fictional being who was as real, if not more real, than actual people in her life. Her novel *One of Ours,* for example, was inspired by the death of her cousin G. P. Cather in World War I; he became the model for Claude, a young boy from Nebraska who dies a heroic death in France. During the writing of the novel, Cather felt Claude's presence all around her: he was always with her, she told her friend Dorothy Canfield Fisher. It was hard to finish the novel because it would mean ending her relationship with him. Writing to Ferris Greenslet of her decision to leave Houghton Mifflin, Cather said, "I am leaving your firm for Claude's health," as if she were a mother protecting a child. Cather had felt an equally intense bond with Thea Kronborg. She told Elizabeth Sergeant that "it was as if Thea lived in her own right, objectively, and was not a creation of hers: she depended on Thea to such an extent that when the book came out and the close inner tie was severed, she felt the pang and emptiness of one deserted." Often, the tie with a novel and character persisted after the book was published, and Cather would refer to the novel as "he" or "she," depending on the gender of the main character, as opposed to "it."

When Cather was an undergraduate, she declared that all artists must suffer "isolation," enduring the "loneliness which besets all mortals who are shut up alone with God." But as we can see, in reality the creative process for Cather was interwoven, in a variety of ways, with personal relationships—with people in her social world, in her imaginative world, and in the world of memory. Creativity was a "gift from heart to heart," Cather wrote in an essay on Sarah Orne Jewett, her image suggesting both emotion and connection as central to the writing process. She could have made the same comment about herself.

One other form of human response can affect the creative process, and at times unpleasantly: the assessments critics and reviewers make of a writer's work. Positive, sympathetic reviews can encourage a writer to continue; negative or hostile ones may contribute to blocking or silencing the creative process. After her novel *The Awakening* was published to almost universally condemning reviews, Kate Chopin wrote very little and never published another novel. By contrast, Cather received such strong early reviews for her first novels that she had the confidence to challenge Houghton Mifflin on the basis of them. During the 1930s, however, she became increasingly subject to critical attacks. Why did this happen, and what was her response?

Beginning with *O Pioneers!,* Cather did not write to please an external audience, and so the independence and freshness of her voice pleased critics who saw her as a promising, vigorous young writer. Impressed with the "extraordinary reality" he found in *My Ántonia,* the critic and man of letters H. L. Mencken became Cather's particular champion. Prominent critics such as Randolph Bourne, Heywood Broun, and Carl Van Doren linked Cather with Theodore Dreiser

WILLA CATHER

(*Sister Carrie*) and Sherwood Anderson (*Winesburg, Ohio*) as writers bringing a new realism to American letters. In the first major assessment of Cather in a literary history, *Contemporary American Novelists: 1900–1920,* Carl Van Doren compared her favorably with her mentor Sarah Orne Jewett, claiming that the "thin, fine gentility" of Jewett's world faded beside the "rich vigor" of Cather's pioneer fiction, whose "spaciousness" and epic sweep ranked her with writers like Walt Whitman. Noting that Cather's epics featured female heroes, Van Doren nevertheless found them able to represent a universal American story: "The struggle of some elected individual to outgrow the restrictions . . . of numbing circumstances."

Endorsed by such important cultural authorities, Cather enjoyed a steadily rising reputation throughout the 1920s: she won the Pulitzer Prize for *One of Ours* in 1923; she was granted honorary degrees from Yale, Columbia, and the University of Michigan; she was invited to prestigious writers' colonies such as Bread Loaf and MacDowell; she was elected to the National Institute of Arts and Letters in 1929; she was awarded the American Academy of Arts and Letters Howells Medal for *Death Comes for the Archbishop* in 1930. Further evidence of Cather's firm position as a major contemporary writer was the selection of *Death Comes for the Archbishop* by the College Entrance Board as a text for high school students to prepare; this was sound cause for congratulation, Ferris Greenslet informed Cather, because selection meant that a book had been established as an American classic.

By the end of the 1920s, Cather seemed to be firmly established as a major writer whose works had attracted both critical and popular acclaim. Yet hints of the attacks to come in the 1930s can now be seen in the negative, even hostile reviews of *One of Ours* (1922), which pleased the Pulitzer Prize committee but not the reviewers. The book was generally dismissed by male reviewers as a woman writer's romanticized, outmoded view of combat. It was, H. L. Mencken charged in his 1922 review, evidently using the worst epithet he could imagine, very like the work of a "lady novelist." For the first time, Cather was explicitly judged as limited because of her gender. Most reviewers and critics were men, not women, of letters, and they thought Willa Cather

THE WRITING LIFE

Cather (second from left) chats with former employer S. S. McClure (left) in Gramercy Park in New York City.

should not have attempted a war novel—that was a man's subject. Perhaps, some reviewers suggested, Cather's imagination was a trifle limited, a little, well, feminine.

Critical attacks did not emerge again until the 1930s, the decade when American society was rived by the economic collapse of the depression. American writers and intellectuals flirted openly with socialism and communism; the economic and social ills seemed so grave that only a fundamental restructuring of society could ease oppression and poverty. Many literary people felt that writers should address such problems in their work, giving readers both powerful images of injustice and hope for change. In this cultural climate, John Steinbeck's *The Grapes of Wrath,* which exposed the exploitation of migrant workers in California, was the kind of novel that was highly praised.

Although Cather's novels continued to be praised by journals such as *Saturday Review* and *Commonweal,* a Catholic publication, they found increasing disfavor with left-wing critics who believed art should grapple with the stern social, political, and economic realities of the time. Looking at Willa Cather's work, instead of finding embattled Nebraska farmers fighting railroad interests or women sweatshop workers organizing, they saw Catholic missionary priests in the 19th-century Southwest (*Death Comes for the Archbishop*), 17th-century French settlers in Quebec (*Shadows on the Rock*), and a romantic young woman coming of age (*Lucy Gayheart*). They were not pleased. Such subjects struck them as escapist and romantic. Cather wrote, complained Newton Arvin in the *New Republic,* as if "mass production and technological unemployment and the struggle between the classes did not exist," and so she had failed to "come to grips with the real life of her time."

In 1933, Granville Hicks published "The Case Against Willa Cather" in the *English Journal,* equating Cather's literary decline with what he considered her growing conservatism. Instead of dealing with the sordid present, she was fleeing to an idealized past, he charged. She was an escapist writer guilty of flabby romanticism, and because she could no longer examine "life as it is," she did not deserve to be considered one of America's great writers. She was, Hicks decided, becoming second class.

From one perspective, the attacks on Cather reflect a conflict over art and politics. Critics such as Hicks, in assuming that all art must conform to a certain definition of the political, were disregarding the important truth Cather had discovered about the creative process: that writers must write from a deep inner source. And such critics ignore the ways in which all art in fact is political, if we make our definition of political more rich and complex.

In fact, we can now look back at what can be called Cather's "Catholic" or "conservative" novels, *Death Comes for the Archbishop* and *Shadows on the Rock,* and can see them as offering radical challenges to some dominant American values. Hostile to the shallow materialism and worship of technology she saw overtaking 20th-century American life, Cather was drawn in these novels toward traditional societies in which the values of community, ritual, and storytelling were honored. Whether this is a "conservative" or a "radical" view very much depends on the context within which a work is written, read, and reviewed. Looking at these novels from the vantage point of the 1990s, I see them as radical in suggesting that technological or material progress may not

THE WRITING LIFE

be the highest human goal, but to Granville Hicks and others they seemed unforgivably apolitical.

On the surface, the attacks on Cather in the 1930s seemed connected with the economic politics of class. But sexual politics was also at work here as male critics, confronted with a woman writer a previous generation of reviewers had defined as major, tried to cut her down to size. Throughout the 1930s and 1940s, critics hostile to Cather not only referred to her as a "feminine" writer; they also established a set of metaphoric equivalences among "feminine," "romantic," "sentimental," "soft," and "small"—a circle of associations that led them, seemingly inevitably, from "woman" to "minor writer." Lionel Trilling thought Cather's "mystical concern with pots and pans" in *Shadows on the Rock* plummeted her fiction to the embarrassing level of the *Woman's Home Companion*. Seemingly kinder, Alfred Kazin used imagery of

Cather receives an honorary degree as a Doctor of Letters from Princeton University in 1931. She was the first woman ever to receive an honorary degree from Princeton.

diminishment in *On Native Grounds* (1942), when he declared that if Cather's "world became increasingly elegiac and soft, it was riches in a little room." Subscribing to an unstated assumption that masculine values and worlds were aesthetically superior to feminine ones, such critics influenced the summing up of Cather's achievement made by Henry Canby in the influential *Literary History of the United States* (1948). Canby clearly contrasts Cather and Sinclair Lewis as a female and male writer and suggests that the feminine is literarily inferior to the masculine: "Her art was not a big art. It does not respond to the troubled sense of American might and magnitude realized but not directed, and felt so strongly by such men as Sinclair Lewis in the same decades. It is national in significance, but not in scope. Her colleagues among the men 'sweated sore' over that job, whereas her books rise free and are far more creative than critical. She is preservative, almost antiquarian, content with much space in little room—feminine in this, and in her passionate revelation of the values which conserve the life of the emotions."

Canby's assessment is what we can call damning with faint praise. From our current perspective, we can see the sexist and patriarchal assumptions behind his vision of "big" sweating male writers laboring to produce important novels equal to America's "might and magnitude." Meanwhile, delicate, hardly perspiring female writers such as Cather allowed books to waft freely upward from their pens—smaller, lighter, air-filled books that took as their subject that very narrow slice of life, "the life of the emotions."

Given our different critical assumptions and aesthetic views, critics in the 1990s, male and female alike, view Willa Cather as a major writer whose work, far from being escapist, took as its subject the connection between art and life. And most contemporary critics would not agree with Canby that the "life of the emotions" is a limited subject. Nor would they agree that Cather's fiction did not equal the scope of American life; on the contrary, contemporary readers see Cather as one of our most complex, innovative, and far-reaching novelists.

But Cather could not foresee the reemergence of her literary stature in the 1980s and 1990s. In the 1930s, she only knew that her

THE WRITING LIFE

work was being attacked in some important quarters, and that it had something to do with her gender. The critics were cursing her, she wrote to fellow novelist Sinclair Lewis, because she did not write like a man.

Faced with external criticism, Cather could have tried to please the reviewers and write against her own grain. But she kept to her own course, as Sarah Orne Jewett might have advised. Cather's last novel, *Sapphira and the Slave Girl,* published in 1940, was set in 19th-century Virginia and concerned the tangled relationships among a group of women—a slaveholding mother, her daughter, and the slave girl whose escape the daughter aids. Reading this novel now, when we are attuned to questions of race and gender, we can see how daring a novel *Sapphira* was. But Cather was publishing a novel centered on women and set in the 1850s, and she must have known this would not please her critics. She wrote the story she had to tell, however, trusting the integrity of her unconscious, not letting Granville Hicks's scolding voice prevent her from speaking in her own.

The independence Cather showed in writing *Sapphira* during her troubled critical decade is also evident in the novel's unusual form. We read what seems to be a conventional historical novel, but then at the end we turn to an "Epilogue." Instead of continuing the novel's fiction, the "Epilogue" is a personal essay in which Cather tells the story of the real-life event that gave rise to her novel—the reunion she witnessed between a mother and daughter. The daughter had escaped from slavery, fleeing from Virginia to Canada, and in the late 1870s the young Cather was present when the daughter returned and saw her mother for the first time in more than 15 years.

In a sense, Cather ends her last novel by telling, in her own voice, the story of her creative process: the childhood memory of the mother-daughter reunion gave rise to her last novel. This mixing of genres, of fiction and memoir, was then a daring move, although one that is more common today, when many American writers are blurring the lines separating the novel from autobiography and memoir. But this was not the case in 1940. And because Cather was being criticized for being too limited and feminine, it was brave indeed for her to risk disapproval or

WILLA CATHER

Cather (far left) and poet Edna St. Vincent Millay (second from left) are honored by a French literary society in 1933. Cather proved to be an amazingly prolific writer, producing a new novel every year or two throughout the 1920s and 1930s.

even ridicule by ending her novel with an autobiographical narrative. She was a private person and she was writing in a critical climate that did not encourage self-exposure. Yet it seemed to her that her fiction demanded a personal conclusion, and she did what she felt her material required.

Cather may have found some support for her continued creative risks not only from her friends, family, and publisher, but also from people whom she valued more than critics: ordinary readers of her work. During the last years of her life, Edith Lewis tells us, Cather took increasing pleasure in her correspondence with readers from all over the world. "Letters that were truly from 'the people,' not from any particular class of people, bringing to her their gratitude, their homage, their affection, in the kind of language she most appreciated—the language art cannot invent—were a sort of giving back to her, a return in kind, of the qualities of feeling she had herself expended in her writing career." Although, sadly, we do not have these letters, Lewis

THE WRITING LIFE

selected some quotations to suggest their range and quality: "I would love to count myself your friend." "Your books have somehow helped me, a boy from Wisconsin, to take heart again in my effort to rebuild my health and life." "I am glad you are alive, and have written so many splendid books." Finding a "great anonymous affirmation" of her art in the private voices of her readers, Cather tried to answer each letter personally. These heartfelt, honest letters from readers helped her to cope with her critics, and they may also have helped her to accept the loss and grief that became more and more a part of her life throughout the 1930s and 1940s.

Writing to her friend Zoë Akins in 1932, Cather said that after one was 45 years old, it simply rained death around one; after 50, the rain became a storm. Cather was then 59 and had recently suffered the deaths of both her parents. Her father died of a heart attack in 1928, and her mother died in 1931 after much suffering. Virginia Cather had a stroke in 1928 that left her paralyzed and almost speechless. Cather had traveled back and forth to California, where her mother was in a sanatorium, for more than two years. She would stay several weeks for each visit; when she left, she would be so emotionally devastated by her mother's pain and helplessness that she could not write.

Then, in 1935, Cather had to face another loss: Isabelle McClung, who had a fatal kidney disease, had come to New York for treatment. Cather spent most of her time caring for Isabelle, and later that year she visited Isabelle in Paris, probably knowing this might be the last time she would see her most loved friend. It was. Isabelle died in 1938, and Cather's grief kept her from working for months. Her brother Douglass died the same year.

Cather found some compensation for her losses in her writing, after she had recovered enough from grieving to be able to work. The deaths of her parents even liberated aspects of her creativity: she was able to draw on these powerful bonds in her writing more directly than she had before. Her portrait of the gentle pharmacist Euclide Auclair in *Shadows on the Rock* draws on memories of her father. And in "Old Mrs. Harris," written after her mother's death, Cather wrote her most autobiographical short story, featuring a grandmother, mother, and daughter. The story, which is filled with sympathy for the mother's point of view, also acknowledges the similarities between strong-minded mother and stubborn daughter—"Dat Vickie is her mother over again," observes a neighbor. Most likely Cather's loss of her mother inspired her to recapture her in art. And the fact that her mother could no longer be a reader of her fiction liberated creative energies that would also give rise to her last novel, *Sapphira and the Slave Girl.*

Cather had to face another loss that in some ways was even more debilitating than the deaths of parents and friends: the loss of her health as she confronted her own aging and death. Cather had always found her own illnesses very difficult to bear. Valuing strength and self-assertion, she disliked herself when she was weak or ill, as if the illness were somehow her fault and caused her to lose self-respect. Writing her childhood friend Irene Miner in 1942 after a long hospital stay,

(From left to right) S. S. McClure, Cather, novelist Theodore Dreiser, and actor Paul Robeson gather at a 1944 ceremony given by the American Academy of Arts and Letters, the organization that had honored Cather with a Howells Medal in 1930 for *Death Comes for the Archbishop.*

THE WRITING LIFE

Cather told her how she hated to be sick: illness made her feel defective. Cather liked to be in control of people and events and herself, and her inevitable loss of control when ill placed her back in the dependent female role she thought she had left behind.

Throughout her last two decades, Cather was particularly plagued by injuries to her hand and arm. In 1935, she sprained the tendons in her right wrist and would suffer a recurring inflammation, often having to wear a brace. She was frequently in pain and found writing an agony. Understandably, Cather's literary output slowed during her last years: she published *Lucy Gayheart* in 1935, *Sapphira and the Slave Girl* in 1940, and then worked only sporadically on short stories and an unfinished novel until her death in 1947.

"The world broke in two in 1922 or thereabouts," Willa Cather once said, claiming she belonged to the "former half." She was referring to her increasing distaste for a modernizing American culture she found materialistic and soulless. But if we take the phrase another way, it can help us understand the difference between the first and the second half of Cather's life.

During the first half of life, she was living what we might call the child's story. Looking ahead toward individual accomplishment, she saw life as an ascending curve, seemingly without end, or ending in the drama of personal success. But once Cather attained the individual success she had sought and entered the second half of life—in my view, after she published *The Song of the Lark,* entered her mid-forties, and suffered the loss of Isabelle in marriage—she saw that the end of life was not individual accomplishment but death, the final obliteration of the self. This was, to say the least, a sobering realization, and it is one that comes to many people in midlife.

Cather's response was to continue to tell stories in the face of death, writing novels that became more and more unconventional in structure. Early novels such as *O Pioneers!* and *The Song of the Lark* told variations of what we might call the hero's plot—linear, chronological narratives in which an exceptional individual triumphs over hostile or restrictive circumstances. But beginning with *My Ántonia,* Cather began to tell different kinds of stories—novels in which individual achievement is not as important as the human impulse to tell stories. "Whatever we had missed," Jim Burden reflects, "we possessed together the precious, the incommunicable past." But it is Jim's triumph that he has managed to tell the story of the "incommunicable past" in the account he has written of Ántonia.

Cather's later work, following the break in her world, admits much more darkness and limitation than her early novels. Claude dies in World War I; Myra Henshawe faces a lonely and poverty-ridden old age in *My Mortal Enemy;* Godfrey St. Peter resigns himself to a limited domestic existence in *The Professor's House;* the archbishop does not live to see his cathedral built in *Death Comes for the Archbishop.*

But Cather's last novels in a way are more satisfying than her early ones. While they acknowledge the darkness that is part of human life, they also celebrate the light. And the light in her work is the power of stories which take many forms in her later work: they can be the simple conversations farm people have with each other, as in "Neighbor Rosicky"; the different myths and religions that structure the worlds of the Native Americans, Mexicans, and Anglos in *Death Comes for the Archbishop;* the rituals of cooking and housekeeping that are passed down from mother to daughter in *Shadows on the Rock;* the music that inspires Lucy Gayheart; and the inherited folktales and legends that Cather received from the old women in Virginia and that gave rise to *Sapphira and the Slave Girl.*

In these novels, Cather realizes that there is no one story or belief system that is universally true; there is no one way of shaping reality. But time and again her imagination is drawn to people's need to transcend the limitations of their own selves by sharing in a narrative that is communal, a narrative that allows them to connect to something beyond the self.

In her later work, Cather faced her broken world, stared at her own death, and continued to tell stories about how people tell stories in the face of death, how people struggle to be human. Some readers of Cather may prefer earlier and more heroic novels such as *O Pioneers!* and *The Song of the Lark;* perhaps because I am in the second half of life myself, I find more imaginative sustenance from the fiction beginning with *My*

THE WRITING LIFE

The Shattuck Inn in Jaffrey, New Hampshire, was a favorite vacation spot for Cather. She wrote *My Ántonia* there and, according to her wishes, was buried in Jaffrey.

Ántonia, the first of Cather's novels that is marked both by loss and by the power of storytelling.

There are common threads, however, that weave together Cather's more optimistic early fiction and her darker later fiction. In a review essay on Cather's fiction, Dorothy Canfield Fisher declared that the theme of all Cather's work was "escape," and Cather told Fisher she agreed. By "escape" Cather and Fisher did not mean evasion from duty or responsibility: they used the word to mean transcendence, or the escape from limiting circumstances to a purer realm of spirit and meaning. Over and over again, Cather was drawn to characters who found meaning by connecting to something larger than the self. That essence differed—it could be the land, the family, art, religion, community, even, as in the case of Claude Wheeler, a war he believed to be just. And in her last novel, *Sapphira and the Slave Girl,* that essence was freedom, and the slave girl's escape a literal one as she fled from Virginia to Canada.

What Cather meant by "escape" is perhaps best expressed in *Death Comes for the Archbishop,* where we read a beautiful passage describing the liberation and expansion of the human spirit. Cather is describing

WILLA CATHER

Archbishop Latour's love for the air of desert countries like the Southwest—dry, light air that one "could breathe only on the bright edges of the world, on the great grass plains or the sagebrush desert." The desert air for the archbishop is what the Nebraska Divide was for Alexandra, what music was for Thea Kronborg, what storytelling was for Jim Burden, what creativity was for Willa Cather—a force larger than the self, into which the soul expands.

> The air would disappear from the whole earth in time, perhaps; but long after his day. He did not know just when it had become so necessary to him, but he had come back to die in exile for the sake of it. Something soft and wild and free, something that whispered to the ear on the pillow, lightened the heart, softly, softly, picked the lock, slid the bolts, and released the prisoned spirit of man into the wind, into the blue and gold, into the morning, into the morning!

Willa Cather's last years, which coincided with the outbreak of World War II, were not easy ones. Subject to failing health, surrounded

Cather's independence and strength enabled her to break new ground in American fiction. By accepting herself and her experience, she became a pioneer writer, setting her stories in the Midwest and creating strong female characters who defied stereotype as firmly as Cather herself.

THE WRITING LIFE

by loss and death, fearing for the survival of European civilization, she confessed to a friend that sometimes she just did not want to live in the world. Everything seemed to be crumbling around her. She could only write infrequently, given the pain in her right arm. Dictating was impossible; she needed the physical act of writing in order to see the pictures words made. Trying to dictate a novel, she said, was like trying to play solitaire without looking at the cards.

But she and Lewis maintained some of the old rhythms of their life together. They could not travel to Grand Manan during World War II, so they spent summers at the Asticou Inn at Northeast Harbor, Maine, sharing a "charming cottage" with a fireplace in the living room. It often rained torrents, Lewis remembered, but Cather was happy to sit by the fire and read.

During this last period of her life, Cather found the answer to Robert Frost's question in "The Oven Bird": "What to make of a diminished thing?" Her life was diminished, as it is for many people in old age, but she could take satisfaction from the small pleasures of life. She could still make meaning from her day. As Lewis recalled, "In the last year, it was the little things one lived in; the pleasure of flowers; of a letter from an old friend in Red Cloud, the flying visit of a young niece; of playing, perhaps, Yehudi's recording with Enesco of the Mozart Concerto in D major, made when he was a young boy . . . the glory of great poetry, filling all the days. She turned almost entirely to Shakespeare and Chaucer that last winter, as if in their company she found her greatest content, best preferred to confront the future."

Willa Cather died from a cerebral hemorrhage on April 24, 1947. Edith Lewis carried out her wishes, and she was buried in Jaffrey, New Hampshire, within sight of Mount Monadnock. The inscription on her gravestone reads: "The truth and charity of her great spirit will live on in the work which is her enduring gift to her country and all its people." Below the inscription is a quote from *My Ántonia,* one of Willa Cather's many gifts to us:

> . . . that is happiness, to be dissolved into something complete and great.

Books by Willa Cather

1903	*April Twilights*
1905	*The Troll Garden*
1912	*Alexander's Bridge*
1913	*O Pioneers!*
1915	*The Song of the Lark*
1918	*My Ántonia*
1920	*Youth and the Bright Medusa*
1922	*One of Ours*
1923	*April Twilights and Other Poems; A Lost Lady*
1925	*The Professor's House*
1926	*My Mortal Enemy*
1927	*Death Comes for the Archbishop*
1931	*Shadows on the Rock*
1932	*Obscure Destinies*
1935	*Lucy Gayheart*
1936	*Not Under Forty*
1940	*Sapphira and the Slave Girl*
1948	*The Old Beauty and Others*
1949	*Willa Cather on Writing*
1966	*The Kingdom of Art: Willa Cather's First Principles and Critical Statements, 1893–1896,* edited by Bernice Slote
1970	*Willa Cather's Collected Short Fiction, 1892–1912,* edited by Virginia Faulkner; *The World and the Parish: Willa Cather's Articles and Reviews, 1893–1902,* edited by William M. Curtin
1973	*Uncle Valentine and Other Stories: Willa Cather's Uncollected Short Fiction, 1915–1929,* edited by Bernice Slote
1987	*Willa Cather in Person: Interviews, Speeches, and Letters,* edited by L. Brent Bohlke

FURTHER READING

Bennet, Mildred. *The World of Willa Cather*. Rev. ed. Lincoln: University of Nebraska Press, 1961.

Bloom, Harold, ed. *Ántonia*. New York: Chelsea House, 1991.

———. *Willa Cather*. New York: Chelsea House, 1986.

———. *Willa Cather's "My Ántonia."* New York: Chelsea House, 1987.

Jewett, Sarah Orne. *The Country of the Pointed Firs and Other Stories*. Edited by Willa Cather. New York: Doubleday, 1956.

Lewis, Edith. *Willa Cather Living*. New York: Knopf, 1953.

O'Brien, Sharon. *Willa Cather: The Emerging Voice*. New York: Oxford University Press, 1987.

Sergeant, Elizabeth. *Willa Cather: A Memoir*. Lincoln: University of Nebraska Press, 1963.

Chronology

1873	Born Wilella Sibert Cather on December 7, near Winchester, Virginia, to Charles Fectigue Cather and Mary Virginia Boak Cather
1884	Moves with her parents to a ranch in Webster County, Nebraska
1885	Moves with family to Red Cloud, Nebraska
1890	Cather moves to Lincoln to complete preparation for entering the University of Nebraska
1891–95	Attends University of Nebraska; meets, befriends, and breaks with Louise Pound
1896–97	Goes to Pittsburgh to work as editor for *Home Monthly,* a traditional women's magazine
1897–1901	Works as newspaper editor and drama critic for the Pittsburgh *Leader*
1899	Meets Isabelle McClung
1901–2	Teaches English and Latin at Central High School in Pittsburgh
1903	Publishes *April Twilights,* a collection of poetry
1903–6	Teaches at Allegheny High School in Pittsburgh
1905	Publishes first collection of short stories, *The Troll Garden*
1906–12	Moves to New York City to join editorial staff of *McClure's Magazine*
1908	Moves into apartment with Edith Lewis, who becomes Cather's lifelong companion; meets writer and mentor Sarah Orne Jewett
1912	Publishes *Alexander's Bridge,* her first novel; makes first of many voyages to the American Southwest

1913	Publishes *O, Pioneers!,* her first novel set in the Midwest, to great acclaim
1915	Publishes *The Song of the Lark;* Isabelle McClung announces upcoming marriage to violinist Jan Hambourg
1918	Cather publishes the highly successful novel *My Ántonia*
1920	Switches publishers, from Houghton Mifflin to Alfred A. Knopf; publishes collection of short stories *Youth and the Bright Medusa*
1922	Publishes the World War I novel *One of Ours*
1923	Wins Pulitzer Prize for *One of Ours;* publishes *A Lost Lady*
1925	Publishes *The Professor's House*
1926	Publishes *My Mortal Enemy*
1927	Publishes southwestern historical novel, *Death Comes for the Archbishop*
1928	Cather's father dies
1929	Cather elected to the National Institute of Arts and Letters
1930	Wins American Academy of Arts and Letters Howells Medal for *Death Comes for the Archbishop;* Cather's mother dies
1931	Cather publishes *Shadows on the Rock*
1932	Publishes collection of short stories, *Obscure Destinies*
1935	Publishes *Lucy Gayheart*
1936	Publishes essay collection *Not Under Forty*
1938	Isabelle McClung dies
1940	Cather publishes *Sapphira and the Slave Girl*
1947	Dies at her home in New York City on April 24

INDEX

Akins, Zoë, 87, 118, 131
Alexander's Bridge, 89, 90, 95, 96
April Twilights, 30, 73, 75
Ashmore, Ruth, 61
Austen, Jane, 50, 71

Back Creek, Virginia, 27, 29, 30, 38
Boak, Rachel (grandmother), 36–37
Bourda, Josephine, 84, 119
Brontë, Charlotte, 50, 71

Carlyle, Thomas, 48, 52
Cather, Caroline (grandmother), 30, 36, 38
Cather, Charles (father), 30, 32, 34, 38, 39, 41, 47, 57, 131
Cather, Douglass (brother), 33, 42, 90, 131
Cather, Elsie (sister), 33, 72
Cather, George (uncle), 38
Cather, Mary Virginia Boak (mother), 32–33, 34, 36, 38, 41, 42, 44, 47, 78, 131
Cather, Roscoe (brother), 33, 42, 103
Cather, Willa Sibert
  awards, 114, 124
  birth, 27, 29, 30
  childhood, 21–27, 29, 106
  college years, 29, 30, 47–53, 63, 65
  critiques of work, 100–101, 102, 111, 113–14, 123–29
  essays, 62, 114, 123
  illness and death, 132–33, 136–37
  Jewett, Sarah Orne, friendship with, 75–81, 95, 123, 124, 129
  journalism, 52–53, 58, 65, 68–69, 73, 74, 80, 101
  literary ambitions, 41, 50, 52–53, 86–87, 95–97
  literary development, 93, 94–99, 102
  medical ambitions, 42–44, 48, 50
  poetry, 30, 67, 73
  publishers, change of, 114–16, 122
  sexuality, 23, 24–25, 26, 27, 34, 42, 49–50, 51, 52–53, 54–59, 61–63, 71–73, 81–85, 99, 108
  short stories, 32, 36, 37, 44, 50, 64, 65, 67, 68, 73, 75, 76, 78, 80, 89, 94–95, 97, 116, 117, 131–32, 133, 134
  teaching career, 69
Cather, William (grandfather), 30, 36, 38

Death Comes for the Archbishop, 37, 91, 97, 113, 114, 124, 126, 134, 135–36
Ducker, Will, 42, 48

Fisher, Dorothy Canfield, 53, 87, 103, 118, 122, 135
Flaubert, Gustave, 38, 72
Fremstad, Olive, 87, 101, 102

Gender issues, 23, 27, 44, 48, 61–62, 71, 93, 97–100, 124, 129
Gere, Mariel, 53, 57, 68
Greenslet, Ferris, 87, 100, 102, 110, 111, 115, 122, 124

Home Monthly, 65, 67, 68, 69

James, Henry, 76, 78, 92, 96, 98
Jewett, Sarah Orne, 61, 75–81, 87, 93, 95, 123, 124, 129

Leader, 68, 69
Lesbianism, 49–50, 57–63, 72, 97, 108
Lewis, Edith, 33, 34, 45, 48, 68, 79, 82–83, 84, 85–86, 87, 104–5, 106, 118, 120, 130, 137
Lewis, Sinclair, 30, 128, 129
Lost Lady, A, 29, 45, 79, 97, 113–14
Lucy Gayheart, 97, 114, 126, 133, 134

McClung, Isabelle, 71–72, 73, 81, 82, 84, 87, 89, 94, 102–4, 110, 118, 131, 133
McClure's Magazine, 69, 73–75, 86, 89, 90, 101

142

My Ántonia, 25, 29, 36, 37, 38, 44, 48, 63, 65, 78, 79, 97, 103, 105, 106–11, 113, 115, 119, 123, 133–34, 137
My Mortal Enemy, 79, 114, 134

Nebraska, 29, 30, 34, 36, 37, 38, 39, 40, 41, 45, 50, 51, 64, 65, 80, 87, 89, 92, 93, 94, 95, 97, 105, 106, 119, 122
New York City, 65, 73, 82, 83, 93, 131
Not Under Forty, 114

Obscure Destinies, 97, 114
"Old Mrs. Harris," 32, 36, 37, 131–32
One of Ours, 71, 97, 113, 122, 124
O Pioneers!, 29, 30, 32, 62, 80, 81, 82, 87, 89, 95, 96, 97, 98–101, 102, 108, 113, 119, 123, 133, 134

"Peter," 44, 65
Pittsburgh, Pennsylvania, 65, 67, 69, 71, 73, 82, 94, 104, 105
Pound, Louise, 49, 52, 53, 54–57, 58, 59
Professor's House, The, 30, 91, 97, 114, 117, 134

Red Cloud, Nebraska, 24, 25, 30, 37, 41, 42, 44, 50, 56, 65, 68, 73, 84, 85, 93, 96, 103, 105, 107, 120, 137
Rich, Adrienne, 58, 97

Sadilek, Annie, 44, 64, 103, 107
Sapphira and the Slave Girl, 34–35, 37, 97, 114, 129, 132, 133, 134, 135
Sergeant, Elizabeth, 78, 83, 86, 87, 95, 103, 118, 119, 121, 123
Shadows on the Rock, 32, 97, 114, 126, 127, 131, 134

Song of the Lark, The, 42, 48, 63, 82, 93, 97, 101, 102, 108, 113, 119, 133, 134
Steffens, Lincoln, 73, 74

Tarbell, Ida, 73, 74
Thomas, Elmer, 24, 25
Troll Garden, The, 73, 75, 80, 116

University of Nebraska, 47, 48, 49, 52, 53, 107

Virginia, 29, 33, 34, 36, 37, 38, 39, 45, 105, 135

Willa Cather Living (Lewis), 84

Youth and the Bright Medusa, 113, 116

Sharon O'Brien is Associate Professor of English and American Studies at Dickinson College. She is the editor of the Library of America edition of the works of Willa Cather and the author of *Willa Cather: The Emerging Voice.*

Martin Duberman is Distinguished Professor of History at the Graduate Center for the City University of New York and the founder and director of the Center for Gay and Lesbian Studies. One of the country's foremost historians, he is the author of 14 books and numerous articles and essays. He has won the Bancroft Prize for *Charles Francis Adams* (1960); two Lambda awards for *Hidden from History: Reclaiming the Gay and Lesbian Past,* an anthology that he coedited; and a special award from the National Academy of Arts and Letters for his overall "contributions to literature." His play *In White America* won the Vernon Rice/Drama Desk Award in 1964. His other works include *James Russell Lowell* (1966), *Black Mountain: An Exploration in Community* (1972), *Paul Robeson* (1989), *Cures: A Gay Man's Odyssey* (1991), and *Stonewall* (1993).

Professor Duberman received his Ph.D. in history from Harvard University in 1957 and served as professor of history at Yale University and Princeton University from 1957 until 1972, when he assumed his present position at the City University of New York.

PICTURE CREDITS:
AP/Wide World Photos: p. 127; Bailey/Howe Library, University of Vermont: p. 56; Bettmann Archive: p. 60; Houghton Library, Harvard University: p. 77; Huntington Library, San Marino, California: p. 117; Nebraska State Historical Society: frontispiece, pp. 20, 22, 24–25, 28, 31, 32, 35, 40, 43, 45, 46, 49, 55, 59, 64, 66, 70, 83, 86, 88, 92, 94, 99, 105, 108, 111, 112, 115, 121, 132, 135, 136; Smith College Archives: p. 85; UPI/Bettmann: pp. 125, 130.